Odd Noises From the Barn

Odd Noises From the Barn

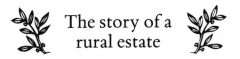 The story of a
rural estate

GEORGE COURTAULD

Secker & Warburg

London

First published in England 1985 by
Martin Secker & Warburg Limited
54 Poland Street, London W1V 3DF

British Library Cataloguing in Publication Data
Courtauld, George
 Odd noises from the barn.
 1. Country life – England – Essex
 2. Essex – Social life and customs
 I. Title
 942.6'70857'0924   DA670.E7

ISBN 0-436-10889-5

Photoset in Linotron 202 Bembo 11/13 pt by
Rowland Phototypesetting Ltd, Bury St Edmunds, Suffolk
and printed in Great Britain by St Edmundsbury Press
Bury St Edmunds, Suffolk

Contents

	ACKNOWLEDGEMENTS	6
1	THE BACKGROUND	7
2	FIRST LESSONS	12
3	HEALTH AND FOOD: GROWTH AND ROUTINE	23
4	NEW NEIGHBOURS: MAN AND BEAST	37
5	BUYING AND SELLING	50
6	BREEDING AND BIRTH	62
7	RIDING AND CONTROL	79
8	A FISHING INTERLUDE	90
9	A BOW AT ANOTHER VENTURE	102
10	DRIVING	116
11	OPEN TO THE PUBLIC	129
12	THE OUTDOOR LIFE	142
13	THE GOURMETS	158
14	THE SHOW	173
	BIBLIOGRAPHY	187

Acknowledgements

Most of the leading characters in this book are based on real people but I have changed many of the names, apart from those of my immediate family.

I would like to thank those people closely associated with this book who have allowed me to use them as the foundations of characters; all the people mentioned in this book whom I have not thanked personally are either dead, or are imaginary.

I have included quite a lot of technical information. For this, I am especially indebted to the following:

Alan Frost, Smith Brothers & Frost, millers;

Jim Waters, The Waters Partnership, Veterinarians.

I also thank the following for their hospitality, mentioned in Chapter 13:

Iain Grahame, Daw's Hall Wildfowl Farm;

Christopher Kerrison, Colchester Oyster Fishery Limited.

CHAPTER 1

The Background

The king desireth not any dowry, but an
hundred foreskins of the Philistines.
I Samuel, 18 xxv

I had often thought that an hundred Philistines' foreskins was a pretty rotten wedding present; little did I know that I was to have an even less pleasing dowry, an hundred ponies. Dominie, my wife, did not bring them with her on our honeymoon, she smuggled the advance guard into our life after a few years of tranquil marriage. The rest followed because she started up a pony stud farm.

I walked into the office of a mill manager one day in time to hear the last words he was bellowing down the telephone:

". . . and finally, I will no longer tolerate these time-wasting outbreaks of sensuality amongst the canteen staff!"

He slammed down the receiver and swivelled on his chair towards me, snorting with exasperation.

"You can't imagine what it's like to be in charge of a weaving shed in this appalling city; in one hour, I have more things to deal with than you'll get in ten years on your peaceful country estate."

I disagreed. "Over the weekend I have had to help to extricate a courting couple jammed between some hay-bales, be midwife to a pregnant pug, de-flea some hedgehogs and expel a neighbour's bull which has fallen in love with one of my sheep. And as for my wife's pony stud, it has problems and happenings of such frequency

and weirdness that your weaving shed is as calm as a convent in
comparison."

This book is mainly the story of those problems and happenings:
how the stud farm developed from a passing whim to a full-time
occupation, the mistakes we made and the lessons we learned, the
strange people we met and the stranger things we had to do. It is
also the story of the farm and estate where all this takes place, and
of the other – often peculiar – ways of making money which we
have tried out, often to pay for the expensive costs of the stud
farm. It is not a children's book, for sex, its planning, undertaking
and results, is the whole theme of a stud farm.

The background is the same as in my last book, but I have
strayed out of the ten acres of the garden into the wider areas of
the estate. The same people continue to be of prime importance in
our community, but I have introduced a larger cast, including
hippies and huntsmen, gypsies and ploughboys, millers and black-
smiths, monks and stable-girls. Although they are of many different backgrounds and occupations, most people who inhabit the
horsey world seem to have two things in common: a slight smell
of horse sweat and an inclination to walk on the outer edges of
their feet so that their legs bow out like nut-crackers.

Amongst the people of our community, only Michael Ryan, the
scrap merchant, is interested in ponies.

"Hello, flower," he says to the latest stable-girl; she titters back in gratification as she toils over the dungle, heaping it anew with yet more muck from the stables. He then wanders over to the nearest stall and pokes his bristly head over the half-door to examine the toothy inhabitant with professional appraisal.

On the other hand, Oscar Monk, the gamekeeper, divides anything that moves into "game" or "vermin", and as I am not allowed to shoot ponies nor he to trap them, he is slightly uncertain of their classification but is inclined, like me, to put them on the vermin list. Tony Crisp, the farm manager and Thomas Bradawl, in charge of estate maintenance, know of them as creatures which continuously knock down their fencing. James Hart, the gardener, likes only two sorts of animals, mongrels and cart horses; he thinks of the ponies as irksome creatures whose hard hooves pock-mark the lawns. Mrs Rutland also has the common-sense opinion of a keen gardener but, being a women, is rather inclined to think of foals as sweet.

Dominie started with three advantages: she had the land, the buildings and the inherited inclination.

Firstly, the land: the heavy wheat-producing fields of the Essex-Suffolk border. It is so heavy and sticky that our local horse, the Suffolk Punch, has been bred without "feathers", the long fringe of hair below the knee that is so noticeable on other British cart horses; attractive, but liable to ball up into great clods with our type of soil. We are proud of this robust quality, and cannot resist a sadistic gloating when visitors from the effete farmlands of Cambridgeshire or Norfolk totter and complain across our Essex plough, huge dollops of mud encasing their trendy green wellies. This clay is hard to work, but productive: it includes some of the best wheat land in Europe. It is therefore not ideally suited for ponies, being too valuable to waste on unprofitable livestock instead of being used for arable farming. However our estate is unlike much of Essex in being hilly. A river and its mile-wide valley bisect the area and brooks have eroded smaller but steeper valleys. Some of the resulting slopes are too steep for combine harvesters. At their feet lie disused water meadows. All these difficult lands are suitable for grazing.

Previously, the richness of the soil, the absence of stone and the bounteous availability of timber resulted in the construction of vast, hall-like barns. Their tarred hulks now lie on the landscape like stranded whales, with broken-backed roofs, ribs showing through rotted walls and with huge, empty, gaping portals. Nasty, alien-looking buildings have taken over. They have cement floors instead of stone flags, asbestos walls instead of weather-boarding and corrugated roofing instead of thatch. Although character-less and intrusive they are ideally suited to modern farming methods and so Dominie had a good choice of the attractive but obsolete buildings which have been replaced by the modern monstrosities.

There is much sense in the cliché, "Look at the mother before you marry her daughter". When I was wooing Dominie I noticed that her mother possessed a flock of pigeons, 14 different species of waterfowl, 3 parrots, a string of race horses, a bevy of bantams, a pride of peacocks, 6 cats, 12 dogs, 7 children, a herd of goats and a husband. I noticed all this with interest rather than unease; the latter emotion began to develop after the birth of our fourth child and the purchase of the sixth dog, but it was not until the arrival of Little Kate and Bumble Bee that the full and dire significance of that cliché dawned upon me.

We had been married for eight years. Henrietta, George and Charlie were all at school, Candy had grown teeth and hair and had begun to read. I commuted to London every day. Dominie started getting restless.

I arrived from the office one dark autumn evening to find the house empty but for Candy, lisping over the adventures of Winnie the Pooh to old Mrs Pipkin, who was babysitting. Where was my dinner? Where was my wife?

"She's gone to get them there foals," cackled the crone who then proceeded to tell me about Mr Pipkin's piles and her "very coarse vines" before I could ask, "What foals?"

The evening wore on. My stomach shrank. Candy began to whinge and the dogs to whine. Mrs Pipkin clanjandered on about disease, death, itchings and arteries.

Dominie finally arrived. Her car was groaning with the effort of pulling a ramshackle box on wheels. I peered inside; two small woolly faces with prick ears and large eyes stared worriedly back.

"This is Little Kate, a filly, and this is Bumble Bee, a colt," said Dominie. I looked at them with mounting disfavour.

"You take the colt by this leading rein, and I'll take Little Kate, and we'll put them in the garage which I've got ready for them."

I suddenly realised that my Lagonda, my pride and joy, a car which had been in the winning team at Le Mans in the 1930s, had been evicted from its home and was skulking beneath a row of yew trees.

As I grumpily led the colt towards his new stable he gently, but firmly, wrapped his forelegs round my waist.

It was symbolic, somehow.

CHAPTER 2

First Lessons

A whip for the horse,
a bridle for the ass,
and a rod for the fool's back.
Proverbs, 26 iii

Welshmen can be contradictory: sudden bursts of jovial singing alternate with long periods of melancholy; they are poetic and romantic, yet strictly puritanical; they have been fiercely independent and individualistic, yet are more socialist than the rest of Britain. Mr Jones, our Welsh immigrant, is as much of an individualist as any of his countrymen, as is particularly evident from his clothing: whatever he is wearing, he always has a neat bowler hat perched on top and a scruffy pair of gym shoes underneath. The latter account for his local name: Dai Plimsoles.

He was leaning through the garage-cum-stable window with his friend, Mr Ryan, inspecting the new arrivals. As Dominie walked up to him he turned and spoke to her with delighted excitement.

"You've got the right breed here," he lilted in the chanting accents of the Vale of Llangollen. "Welsh Mountain Ponies, they are, the most beautiful and the most big-hearted of all the flying-maned ponies that run and graze through the mountains and moorlands of our fair islands and I have several for sale at very good prices." He began running on the spot, a habit of his when excited.

"What is the difference between a horse and a pony?" I asked.

There was an excited Celtic debate between Mr Ryan and Dai but they came to no definite agreement, concluding only that "a pony is definitely different to a horse – it is not just a small horse". Normally, I have since learned, a pony must never be over 14.2 hands, but some Arab horses are less and Welsh cobs can be more. There are differences in conformation: a pony usually has shorter ears and a more compact body than a horse, but a Welsh Mountain Pony is long limbed whilst a Suffolk Punch has the burly build of a heavy working pony. There's something about the poll, the top of the head, which is different: it looks rounder and closer set on a pony.

Horses and ponies have more similarities than differences and Dai Plimsoles lifted up his sing-song voice to recite a list of the qualities of the equine breed. Later, he wrote it down for me, and I reproduce it below. The first version of this was probably written by one of the Fitzherberts, a senior courtier to Henry VIII, but that version had 50 properties, Dai's has been abridged to 30.

A good horse should have these qualities:
3 of a man – bold, proud and hardy;
3 of a woman – a broad breast, round hips and a long mane;
3 of a lion – countenance, courage and fire;
3 of a bullock – the eye, the nostril and the joints;
3 of a sheep – the nose, gentleness and patience;
3 of a mule – strength, constancy and foot;
3 of a deer – head, legs and short hair;
3 of a wolf – throat, neck and hearing;
3 of a serpent – memory, sight and turning;
3 of a hare – running, walking and suppleness.

A further abridgement I know is quoted by Captain Firecrest, a cynical horse-dealer whose sixty years with horses and ponies has led him to expect the following qualities of the average animal that he buys – but apparently not of those that he sells:

3 of a woman – expensive to keep, difficult to mount and often has to be bought new shoes;
3 of a schoolboy – whistles, has chestnuts and a tendency to crib;

3 of a flea – jumps suddenly, bites and won't be boxed;
3 of a crab – sidles, has eyes on stalks and is hard-mouthed;
3 of an ostrich – kicks, has a swan neck and cannot be caught;
3 of a life peer – has hairy heels, coronets and is of unknown
  breeding.

As well as learning the differences between horse and pony, we
had to learn the differences between the breeds and types of pony.
(A "type" is merely a recognised character, such as a cob, hunter
or palfrey, a "breed" is a recognised species which inherits true to
specified properties.) There are many breeds and types throughout
the world, the British Isles has produced the greatest number of
these in proportion to land area. Mr Ryan suggested that we go
with him to the Ponies of Britain Show, for there we would see
all the breeds of British pony in one day and so it would be easier
to compare them.

The aim of Ponies of Britain is to promote the British pony
breeds and to control their quality. There are two shows each year:
one in spring for the stallions and the other in August for mares
and young stock. The former is now held in the Huntingdon
racecourse and the latter at Peterborough, but when Dominie
started with her ponies the shows were both held at Ascot, and so
it was south-westward that Mr Ryan drove us to get our first full
taste of the pony world.

He took us in an ancient truck which he had just bought for
scrap and which he considered had just one more journey left
before it was committed to the shredder. We sat in a row on the
cracked plastic upholstery of the only seat and listened to the
asthmatic engine coughing and wheezing beneath our feet and its
old, tired body clattering and squeaking all round us. The open
back of the truck contained the pale-blue corpses of three broken-
down invalid cars which Mr Ryan had not bothered to unload
before the journey. I had to go to my London office first that day,
and did not know what to expect as I stood neatly be-suited outside
my office door at half past ten, waiting to be picked up. Grave
were my misgivings and profound my sheepishness when the
ramshackle contrivance rattled into Hanover Square, tottered
round the statue of William Pitt and juddered to a halt beside me.
I need not have worried, for as we approached the show I noticed
that many of the vehicles were as eccentric or as scruffy as ours.

. . . . the ramshackle contrivance . . .

Anything to do with horses seems to be preceded with a traffic jam, whether it is on the A24 to Epsom or Dead Cat Lane to the Little Todbury Equestrian Carnival and Old Tyme Fayre. Each jam is dominated by its own specialised vehicles: Bentleys at Goodwood, Mercedes at the Derby, Rolls Royces and horse-drawn vehicles at Ascot, Rovers at the Royal and very old Morrises at the Little Todbury. At the Ponies of Britain the only rule is to be individual. There were little panelled boxes like wheeled kennels being towed by psychedelically painted Chevrolets; vast, ultra-modern horse-boxes with rows of weird seating like a space capsule or a dentist's surgery; tiny cars strained under the weight of huge metal containers resembling mobile Nissen huts. We were stuck behind a trailer which, at first sight, contained a litter of guinea-pigs; a second glimpse revealed them to be a trio of truculent-looking Shetland ponies who kept staring at us and nudging each other and whispering among themselves as do the obnoxious passengers of the school bus I often get stuck behind as I commute to the railway station.

As well as looking at the ponies, Dominie had come to look at different horse conveyances. She needed to buy one in order to carry her stock to the various shows which she considered necessary to promote her pony progeny. She was given much advice that day by Mr Ryan's friends. The most sensible was to buy something light, which opened at both front and back, for there are some animals which can be boxed quite easily but which are reluctant to exit backwards. Moreover, if a horse is difficult to box, it can sometimes be induced to enter if the front is opened and it is able to see right through the trailer. Later, when Dominie had to convey up to six ponies from show to show, she bought a horse-box. It is an old army Bedford lorry which has been fitted with a large wooden container: this not only holds the ponies, it also has a separate room forward which is a combined galley, saloon, tack-room and sleeping cabin. Three people can sleep in the gypsy-style bunk in the "luton", the space above the driving cabin, and two more can sleep on a bed which is made by joining the table top to the benches on either side. It is uncomfortable, but our children love the seedy squalor and crudity of it, and they take particular pleasure in lying on the upper bunk and watching the countryside as we drive along.

It is said that some people grow to look like their dogs, and it seemed to me, during the day at the Ponies of Britain, that the same thing happens with horsey people. I learned the differences between some breeds by looking at their owners or riders: the Shetland people were often small and smiling and had a fuzzy woolliness; the riders of Welsh Ponies had a supercilious and haughty air; unlike most, the cobs had a strong and rather assertive masculine element; Exmoor children did not have "mealy noses" but they, more than the others, seemed to have crumb-covered faces from particularly greedy guzzling through picnic hampers.

Mr Ryan bought a catalogue and was able to take us to a selection of show-rings at the appropriate times so that, by the end of the day, we had seen a good number of all the official native breeds. I have summarised his description of each of these below, but with much editing and some added comment, for Mr Ryan, like all horse lovers, has an over-affectionate eye. When I read up the subject in the horsey books which Father Christmas had given Dominie and the girls, I found this prejudiced affection in all of them. Most books on ponies are hagiographies, so it warmed my heart to read a more cynical and critical book which had belonged to my Great-Great-Great-Grandfather. The contents of this would send the average pony lover reaching, in rage or astonishment, for the hunting crop or the gin bottle, but the book was published in 1831 and the breeds have been greatly improved by selective studwork since then.

This iconoclastic work is called *THE HORSE with a Treatise on draught & a copious index*, and I have quoted its anonymous author's comments below in italics.

There are ten breeds of British native pony, nine official and one unrecognised, all breeds being classified as "Mountain and Moorland".

The HIGHLAND PONY is like many Highlanders, being kindly, gentle and well-mannered, having strong thighs, broad knees and being hardy enough to survive on coarse food and on rough ground; they have superb coats in cold weather. However it *"is far inferior to the Galloway* [a small horse of south Scotland]. *The head is large, he is low before, long in the back, short in the legs, upright in the pasterns, rather slow in his paces, and not pleasant to ride, except at the canter . . . . When these animals come to any boggy piece of ground, they first put their nose to it, and then pat it in a peculiar way with one of their fore-feet, and from the sound and feel of the ground, they know whether it will bear them. They do the same with ice."*

The FELL was originally used for a multitude of purposes: raiding the Scottish border, farming, herding livestock, carrying lead from the mines of the Pennine Range and the Lake District, hunting, trekking and participating in trotting races. These days it is normally used only for the last three activities. It is shaggy, with long hair on its jaw and with plenty of feather about its heels. This somewhat primitive look is emphasised by its tough and strongly built conformation.

The DALE is much like the Fell, but its origins centre around the dales of Northumberland rather than the fells of Westmorland. The dale country is slightly more suitable for draught, and thus the Dale is more of a harness pony than is the Fell, as well as being larger.

The NEW FOREST *"are generally ill-made, large-headed, short-necked, ragged-hipped but hardy, safe and useful; with much of their ancient spirit and speed, and all their old paces. The catching of these ponies is as great a trial of skill, as the hunting of the wild horse on the Pampas of South America, and a greater one of patience."* From these remarks, I reckon that the author owned one of these animals. Vividly I remember

Big Sam, my parents' groom, attempting to catch Polly, my New Forest mare: tip-toeing up to her and cajoling her with a tempting bucket of her favourite food; running after her, cursing and shouting with exasperation; pleading, wheedling, threatening, all to no avail until he turned his back on the creature and stormed out of the paddock – followed by the suddenly acquiescent animal.

The EXMOOR is the most recognisable of all ponies, except the Shetland, for it always has a "mealie" nose as if it has just dipped its muzzle into a bucket of bran. Another recognisable trait discloses its primitive origins: it has an "ice tail", an extra fan of short hairs at the root of the tail which was of some advantage in the frozen wastes of Ice-Age Europe. *"Although generally ugly enough, they are hardy and useful. A well-known sportsman says that he rode one of them half a dozen miles and never felt such power and action in so small a compass before."* Its strength, hardiness and courage are still well-famed: it can carry a beefy, cider-and-cream fattened farmer to the end of a hunt. These virtues resulted in eleven Exmoors being sent to the Falklands, after the expulsion of the Argentinian invaders.

The DARTMOOR PONY *"is larger than the Exmoor, and, if possible, uglier. He is sure-footed, and hardy, and admirably calculated to scramble over the rough roads and dreary wilds of that mountainous district."* Since these somewhat critical remarks were penned the Dartmoor has been refined and has become slightly smaller, but it still has great determination and makes a good pony for a competitive child who likes collecting rosettes.

The SHETLAND PONY is the "Thelwell"-type pony so beloved by all who do not know it. My brother had one called Tom Thumb, it looked rather like a furry tea-cosy. Little children who were unaware of its personality would run up to it, arms outstretched, lisping endearments. According to which end they reached first, they would get a kick or a bite for their misguided affections. Big Sam, who knew it was no toy, treated it as a proper pony and as a result it never misbehaved with him. Probably more people have fallen off Shetlands than off any other ponies. They are usually bought for beginners, but some are so round-bodied that the wretched infants can get no grip with their legs which stick out like a pair of jodhpurred wings at either side. A beginner's pony should be more narrow-bodied, in my opinion. In spite of Tom Thumb's tetchy character, Shetland ponies can be very affectionate.

Many were greatly loved by the miners who found them ideal pit ponies: small but muscular, having a powerful pull because of their short legs and good shoulders, and able to endure harsh conditions.

The LUNDY is another island pony, but is not officially recognised as a separate breed, just as a type. It was created by crossing a few selected sires, of which one was a Galloway, with New Forest mares. The result has developed into a tough, hardy beast with a light build, a good temperament and an ability to jump well.

The CONNEMARA: legend has it that they are the descendants of Arab horses who escaped from their Galway masters and interbred with local ponies: thus they have the Mountain and Moorland virtues of strength and hardiness, combined with the grace and speed of the Arab. They are usefully versatile, being fast and showy when between the shafts, comfortable to ride, and good workers for their Irish masters, carrying loads of peat and seaweed.

The WELSH PONY "*is one of the most beautiful little animals that can be imagined. He has a small head, high withers, deep yet round barrel, short joints, flat legs, and good round feet. He will live on any fare, and can never be tired out.*" Not a single harsh word! Praise indeed for the fastidious author of *The Horse*.

Nowadays the Welsh Pony is divided up into four sections. The Section A pony is the one that Dominie has concentrated on. It is small, never over 12 hands, with a noticeably Arab appearance: a small, neat head with a dished face, graceful, and "with an almost haughty stance" when on the move. It is excellent both as a riding pony and in harness. Its official name is "The Welsh Mountain Pony". Sections B, C and D are known, respectively, as "the Welsh Pony of Riding Type", "the Welsh Pony (Cob type)" and "the Welsh Cob". Basically, they increase in size, power and burliness as they go down the alphabet.

There is a stud farm over the border from us, in Suffolk. It is run by an eminently capable spinster called Pamela Rantipole. Brusque and sensible, yet possessed of an almost schoolgirl innocence, she has a pleasant, somewhat weather-beaten face and an extraordinary voice, deep and vibrant and with two moods: the first, which can be heard when she is talking to a pony, sounds like honey being trickled from a golden jug on to a black velvet cushion, the second, which can sometimes be heard above the humdrum hubbub of a cocktail party, sounds like a goose honking for its mate. Dominie had met her because they both sat on the committee of a local charity; they had got on well together, for Dominie recognised the basic kindness behind the screen of heartiness. So when Dominie decided to start a stud farm she asked if Pamela would come over and give some general advice.

We were all sitting in the kitchen having our mid-morning "bait" when she arrived. Draped in ill-fitting tweeds, which looked as if they had been tailored from old horse-blankets, she wore a battered pork-pie hat pulled well down over her grizzled eyebrows and ornamented with a cavalry badge of a running horse – I think it was of The King's Own Hussars. Her only other ornamentation was a pony club badge which held a battered watch on to her lapel.

"Phew! Jolly parky outside!" she gasped, pushing her hat back with be-mittened knuckles. Taking a mug of tea, she continued, "Good-oh! This'll warm up my poor old bones. No thanks, I won't sit, the seat of my Land-Rover has numbed my rump and anyhow I'd like to scout around your super kitchen." With that, she went questing and prying about "like a terrier in a barn", as Bradawl said later. Finally she tipped a cat out of the only empty chair, plumped down, took a loud gulp from her mug and asked: "Decided on a name for your stud yet?"

Dominie had not. Suggestions were immediately offered.

"Tiny Hooves," said old Mrs Pipkin, who comes to iron.

"Meadow Gates," said Bradawl, perhaps thinking of the fencing he'd put up.

"Meadow Sweet," said Hart, more botanically minded.

"Pony Nuts," said Lesley, a half-witted work-experience girl.

"Prime Pony Products," said Tony Crisp, businesslike.

"Aardvark Stud," said Monk.

"Aardvark?"

"Yes, it will get you first in any reference book."

"What is an aardvark?"

"It is an insectivorous quadruped," said Charlie, who never seems to listen, but who never seems to forget.

"I knew one of them once," broke in Mrs Pipkin angrily. "The varmint. 'Go away,' I used to say to him. 'Go away and keep your hands to yourself,' I'd say. 'I can't help it,' he'd say to me he'd say, 'it's me natural passions, they torment me something cruel, do you come along o' me and be my love,' he'd say to me . . ."

We ignored her, for we knew her mind had been warped when young by the over-indulgent perusal of romantic novels and the intense sermonising of the Reverend Jeremiah Scyllitoe of the chapel of Lady Huntingdon's Connexion.

"Why don't we call it after our farm?" I suggested.

"Not possible," boomed Pamela. "There is already one with the same name somewhere up in Yorkshire."

"How about something typically Essex, then," I persisted, "the Mud-Flats Stud, the Hornbeam, Old King Coel's Stud. What was King Coel's other name?"

"Cunobelin," said Charlie, at once.

"Shakespeare called him 'Cymbeline'," said George, who was about to take "Eng. Lit." as one of his O Levels.

"That sounds nice and Welsh," said Pamela approvingly, "I suppose that they were all Welsh in this part of the world then, come to think of it."

"I knew a Welshman once . . ." shouted Mrs Pipkin.

So it was that the Cymbeline Stud was named. It has been misspelled and mispronounced ever since.

The names of the ponies has been another concern. Dominie decided to prefix every pony name with that of the stud, followed, like a car number-plate, by an alphabetical sequence each year. Her first foal, for example, was called Cymbeline's Antigone. This scheme was no problem in the first years when she had only a few foals and the starting letters were easy, but later, when she had to find up to thirty names beginning with a difficult letter like K, she has had to do a considerable amount of thumbing through reference books and the English/Welsh dictionary. She bought the latter because she had decided that, as much as was sensible, her ponies should have Welsh names. But the Welsh must have tongues as agile as snakes in order to pronounce some of their words. We managed with a few, such as Myfanwy, Caradoc, Gwendolyn and Daffyd but some names we did not even try: Culhwch, Goleuddydd or Gwawl – attempting to pronounce those three makes one pant and foam at the mouth: a reaction not likely to attract any potential buyer or show-ring judge.

Dominie has also used Celtic mythology – Lamri (King Arthur's mare) – other lore and legends, as in Frost-mane (the steed of Night) and, as a last resort, anything which started with the correct letter and seemed pleasant, like Melanie, Miranda and Musketeer.

Whatever they are called, it is the rattling of a bucket full of pony nuts which attracts them, rather than the sound of their names.

CHAPTER 3

Health and Food:
Growth and Routine

My bowels boiled, and rested not.
Job, 30 xxvii

I had Wobbler disease, Swamp fever, a touch of the Megrims and my small intestines had become twisted. My fear-crazed eyes continued to wander over the pages of *Veterinary Notes for Horse Owners*. Mud fever – mummification – mylandris phalerate – myoglobinuria – myomata and myoxomata – I had the lot, or so I thought. Medical books send me all of a-tremble, symptoms are described so vividly and in such detail that they develop within me as I read.

Considering the vast number of diseases and ailments that can infect a pony, I am surprised what little trouble ours have had with ill health. "Prevention is better than cure," as Captain Firecrest habitually but conventionally repeats, and certainly most problems are avoided by the regular visits of the vet and the farrier, together with Dominie's routine – a daily check-up on each animal for its health, a six-weekly dosing for worms and an annual powdering for lice.

The vet and the farrier are the most important regular visitors to the stud.

Mr Whippletree, the vet, is a burly, common-sensical man; a cross between a heavyweight wrestler, a watch-mender and a philosopher. He has to combine the strength of someone able to

heave a corpulent sow to her trotters, with the meticulous nicety
needed for stitching up the Caesarean scar on a hamster's stomach;
and the stoic resignation of someone who has to give an enema to
a bull in the early morning and examine the results of his plumbing
through an electronic microscope in the late evening. Most vets
have their own quirky favourites: one of Mr Whippletree's partners
lives and breathes dogs, the other is devoted to any animal if it
belongs to an old-age pensioner; Mr Whippletree likes farm animals, and particularly admires horses.

"I like animals which you can respect," he told me, "and I
learned to respect the horse when I was a rookie in the army at the
start of the war. My very first job was to deal with some horses
which had been given to the British by some American well-
wishers. These mustangs had sailed from the USA to Liverpool,
but because of the appalling weather, the ship had to lie out to sea
for an extra three days. Throughout that time they had no water.

"I had just joined the Royal Army Veterinary Corps. I had not
yet learned the army definition of a volunteer: 'a man who didn't
understand the question', so I found myself recruited as a mustang
re-victualler. There were three of us squaddies under the command
of Sergeant Ritling, a self-important little cock-sparrow of an
NCO. He had decided that although the priority was to give the
horses water, they would be instructed to drink in an orderly and
military manner. He had the wretched – and very angry – animals
unshipped and herded all the way from the docks, through the
city and up to a hill pasture just outside Liverpool's suburbs. Well,
as I've said, he had decided that these colonial animals would
behave according to the rules as laid down in King's Regulations.
He had installed a small, portable drinking trough out of sight of
the pasture, on the other side of the hill. He stood beside it,
stopwatch in one hand, drill-stick in the other, feet at 45 degrees,
chin in, chest out. 'Right,' he said to us, 'those horses will be led
over the hill in pairs and each pair will have exactly 90 seconds to
drink.' The horses thought otherwise. They had scented the water
and, maddened with thirst, all 400 of them charged out towards
the trough once the paddock gate had been opened for the first
pair.

"I was meant to lead them away from the water and into another
enclosure once their minute and a half was over, so I was standing
by the little sergeant when the whole herd, 800 mad-looking eyes,

sixteen hundred flailing hooves and ten times that number of bared teeth, appeared with a thunderous roar over the crest of the hill.

"Sergeant Ritling remained frozen to the spot for a few seconds, his finger still poised over the starter button of his stopwatch; he was first paralysed with astonishment, then with indignation, finally with terror. His nerve broke, and he was going like a thoroughbred when he overtook me running for the safety of the nearest fence."

Mr Whippletree is sometimes summoned on the advice of Mr Dewbit, the farrier, who comes at regular intervals to inspect the feet of the ponies and to shoe any of them which are being ridden or driven. His advice and examinations are most important; almost a quarter of the veterinary book previously mentioned deals with problems of the feet and legs; much of Mr Dewbit's responsibility is to anticipate or notice any of these problems.

He normally arrives at the crack of dawn. He parks his van in the yard and assembles his portable equipment: a small anvil; a gas-fired forge; neatly aligned, like the fearsome instruments in a dentist's cabinet are the fire tongs and shoe tongs for holding hot metal, the pincers for removing old nails and shoes, the hammer for shaping the shoes and driving and clenching the nails, and the rasp and knives, for trimming and tidying the hooves.

This clinical and precise assemblage is very different from the village smithy of my childhood, just after the war. Its dark recesses were barely lit by the glow of the forge until the smith pumped at the overhead handle which sent the leather lungs of the vast old bellows panting and gasping in a corner. The fire would then flare up and illumine the tackle: the squatting bulk of the anvil, like the graven image of a one-horned god on its wooden altar; the hooks on the walls holding implements, horseshoes, bits of plough and other scrap, all festooned with sooty cobwebs. The grey-stubbled, toothless face of the old smith would glow as he drew out a red-hot piece of iron with his long-handled pincers and plunged it, with a bubbling hiss, into the water trough nearby. I remember the smell: a sharp, sour tang of earthen floor, rust, cinders and sweat.

I also remember a forge in a little village in the mountains of the Massif Central. I often used to stay there with some French cousins when I was a child, and one of my greatest pleasures was to wander down the cobbled alleyways after breakfast and visit Monsieur

Picard, the smith, in his tiny forge. He had colossal biceps and immensely broad shoulders surmounted by a minuscule head, like a coconut. He wore an all-enveloping leather apron and was one of the world's experts at cursing.

He cursed because he had to shoe oxen.

Most horses are resigned to shoeing, all oxen hate it. They struggle and kick as if they are being tormented by a picador's goads and as a result they have to be restrained within the confines of a frame. M. Picard's frame was a long, rectangular construction like the skeleton of a box made of iron girders. There were two rollers at the top, from which straps could be passed under the oxen. The rollers would then be wound, with a cacophony of clicking from ratchets, grunting from the smith and creaking harness from the struggling beast, which was finally hoisted on to tip-hooves. The narrowness of the frame and the semi-airborne state of the ox prevented it from harming the smith, but if its struggles were still too objectionable he could tie the leg he was dealing with to the nearest upright. The only English ox-frame I have seen was much more complicated and had, as its main restraint, head stocks which held the beast by the neck. The frame did not look as efficient as its French counterpart, nor did the English yoke, which included two bows that went round the necks of the oxen, with the result that they could hardly breathe. The French yokes had no bows, but were attached to the horns and foreheads, thus taking full advantage of the strongest muscles, the fighting and goring ones of the neck and shoulder. These French yokes were beautifully carved – almost sculpted – to the size and shape of their individual wearers. When I was last in the village M. Picard told me that there were no oxen left and his only work was repairing tractors. He had about thirty old yokes, which he used as kindling wood; he gave me two pair and I was offered £100 for each of them a year later. I sent a message to M. Picard telling him and got an agonisingly distraught one back saying he had just chopped up his last one.

He also gave me a couple of ox-shoes. There are two per foot, as oxen feet are cloven. They are shaped rather like a skiing glove, the oval main plate going under the hooflet, the thumb being curved over it.

The smith's job was not made any easier by the long memory of oxen, who, like elephants "never forget – an injury". Rider

Haggard, in his *Rural England*, wrote that no bull-keeper should ring his own bull, because of its ability to harbour resentment.

Old Mr Rutland said that in all of his life, which included being a rodeo rider in a circus, being shot down when a rear gunner in a bomber, and carrying explosives and sabotage equipment through occupied Europe for MI6, the time that he felt the greatest fear was one day when, as a gaucho in the Argentine, he was sent out into the Pampas to shoot a rogue bull. He was stalking it through the long grass when he heard a stealthy rustle behind him. He looked round and saw, six paces away, on its knees and with its eyes glaring into his, the bull, stalking him.

In comparison to M. Picard, Mr Dewbit's job seems almost sissy: he and the ponies lean comfortably against each other, the upturned pastern resting lightly above his knee while he scours, probes, pares, files and hammers with no apparent concern from the animal. Mr Dewbit only shoes the riding and driving ponies, but all of them need their hooves trimmed and shaped about four times a year, otherwise they grow too long, or misshapen, or they fray and chip. This suggests to me that the horse originated in a rocky area where hooves would be ground down during the animal's travels; similarly, the relatively small stomach and milling action of the teeth suggest a grain eater rather than a grazer.

Mr Dewbit is extremely popular with the dogs for there are few things dogs like better than chewing on a hoof paring.

We had had a tempest one night and Tony Crisp, Tom Bradawl and I were busy with chain saws clearing up a Lombardy poplar which had been blown across the road.

A small car dashed round the corner and screeched to a halt about two feet from the fallen bole: the female driver within sat glowering petulantly through the window, drumming elegantly manicured fingers on the custom-built steering wheel and occasionally revving her engine in a meaningful manner. Finally she stuck her head out of the window and gestured to us with beckoning flips of her hand. Bradawl, who was nearest, went over.

"Here you, when are you going to be finished?" she said in a somewhat quacking voice. Bradawl, who is a patient and polite man, replied soothingly.

"All in good time."

"That's not good enough; who's the boss here?" Bradawl pointed at me; I reluctantly turned off my saw, which hates being restarted, and scowled over.

"Look here, my man, I haven't got all day to wait. Can't you work harder? I know the Chief Constable and the Lord Lieutenant, you know."

"We could work harder, but we don't want to," I replied disagreeably then, slightly ashamed of my rudeness, continued, "we're all doing this voluntarily, rather than wait for the council. Where do you want to go, I may be able to suggest another route?"

"A pony stud with some ridiculous name: 'Kymberline', or something. Just started up by a brewer's daughter."

The way she laid stress to her last two words suggested that she was as impressed with the occupation of Dominie's father as my Moslem friend, Harith, is with an itinerant peddler of pork sausages.

I told her an alternative way and then spent ten enraging minutes trying to restart my saw. When the job was over and we had returned home, I strolled into the kitchen and saw Dominie standing by the oven. She spoke.

"Do you know Monique Fewmet?"

Being somewhat fuzzy and stupid from my efforts with the saw, I did not realise that this question was also an introduction, so brightly replied, "No. She must be the wife of that bat-eared little commuter who's just taken Hempseed Hall. Almost always blotto when he takes the train home, I'm not surprised, I hear his wife . . ."

I trailed to a faltering stop, quelled by the aghast expression on Dominie's face. I turned around and saw, lurking by the window, the woman I had met earlier. She was looking at me with icy indignation.

"Oh! Fewmet! I thought you said Hewett!" I cried unconvincingly, but face-savingly.

"Mrs Fewmet has also just started up a pony stud," said Dominie in a trembly voice. "She's just been round to have a look at ours. I'm afraid our stables sound rather small and scruffy in comparison to hers."

Much of the untidiness which Monique Fewmet had so scorned was my fault, for I had persuaded Dominie to use some rather messy helpers to keep down the pests and vermin. These assistants were the spider, the bat, the swallow, the owl, the chicken and the cow.

I have always disliked spiders: most people have a species of animal which is their own particular *bête noire*: usually these are reptiles, snakes or lizards, but I have never been repelled or alarmed by these. But spiders have always filled me with loathing: all those legs, those protuberant and shifty-looking eyes, above all, the disgusting way they fastidiously parcel up their terror-ridden victims into neat packages as if they were considerately wrapping them up for Oxfam rather than immobilising them so as to suck out their living juices later. However, I am not particularly enamoured of flies either: they, too, have disgusting eating habits; they walk about maddeningly on top of my head with their tickly feet and remind me that I have lost most of my hair; they are potential carriers of disease and parasites. The fly family includes such pests as the ox-warble fly and bot fly, whose repulsive larvae-children live on the flesh and blood of their unwilling hosts; maggot-layers such as green and blue bottles; biters such as horse flies and irritators such as cluster flies which gather round the eyes and mouth. Most of these flies are attracted by the presence of dung heaps, many are also attracted by the smell of livestock. Dominie bustled about her stables housekeeping: sweeping floors, white-washing walls, dabbing disinfectant here and Stockholm tar there; applying broom and duster wherever they could be whisked or wiped. In spite of all this her stables had flies. Occasionally Dominie would miss a corner for a couple of days and a cobweb would be woven in it; the weaver, gorged fatly on stable flies, would grow to horrific proportions in the middle of its net. I eventually managed to persuade Dominie that these spiders' webs were a useful, though scruffy, assistance, so now we have a large and repulsive team of eight-legged helpers which keep up the hygiene standards that Mr Whippletree recommends.

More flies are kept down by swallows and bats. When we built an extension on to our house, I feared that the displacement of our roof timbers would drive away our fellow-residents. I need not have worried: the swallows and bats moved happily into the rafters of the newly-built stables and, less welcome, but still tolerated as we felt that they were part of our community, the hornets moved sixty feet and built a new nest in an undisturbed part of the roof.

We have no owls nesting in the out-buildings near the house, which are too crowded and noisy, but Bradawl put owl-boxes up in most of the other barns of the estate and the result was a satisfactory elimination of rats and mice and their accompanying diseases; less practical, but even more pleasing, is the frequent sight of pale phantoms flitting through the twilit shapes of hedgerow trees.

Our last unpaid assistants were the chickens and cows.

Herbivores are clean eaters, unlike carnivores which eat each other together with their internal parasites. However, when a herbivore voids a parasite, or its egg or larvae, it is likely to be taken in by one of its fellow-grazers. We have about thirty chickens, bantams of mixed breeds, and also a dozen guinea-fowl. They are all insatiably greedy and when not digging up the seeds planted by Hart they are nibbling the tops off flower buds or are all of a-bustle and a-pecking in the stable yard or home paddocks or dungles, eating, one hopes, the parasites and their eggs which can be found amongst the litter. The gritty contents of their gizzards then grind these into a pulp. There can be a disadvantage with poultry: our own chickens are clean and can thus associate with the ponies, but some fowl have mites which can set up a maddening itch on other animals, including humans and horses.

There are two good reasons why cattle and horses can be pastured out with mutual advantage. The first is because of their different grazing methods – the cow uses its tongue as its main implement, wrapping it around tussocks and tall herbage and wrenching its food out of the ground, whereas the horse uses its front teeth to shear and mow the shorter grasses left or created by the cow. The second is because each species destroys some of the other's parasites by eating them and killing them with their differing methods of digestion; the cow being particularly destructive to red worms, a most unpleasant but quite common parasite of the equine breed which sucks blood from the walls of the intestines.

It was for these reasons that we bought Primrose and Buttercup, two Guernsey cows. They scorned the ponies as flibbertigibbets and ignored their cavortings and prancings, preferring to wander slowly and sedately over the pastures like a pair of cloud-shadows. We sent them off to be serviced by Jock, the Highland bull belonging to my brother-in-law, Hamish. Jock had gained local notoriety by raping twenty-seven neighbouring heifers in one night: Hamish said he never knew what gardeners meant by the term "pricking-out" until he saw Jock's busy concentration as he dealt with the compliant herd of maidens queuing up for him in the field next door. Our calves were also useful as scavengers and later, though I never dared tell the children, as cutlets, chops, joints and sirloins.

Although we have usually been trouble-free of disease, we do have one which is almost a local speciality: lock-jaw. Apparently our infestation of the tetanus bacillus is because the soil is amongst the heaviest in Europe and has held the germs which were created by our practice, in medieval times, of intensive pig and sheep rearing. We usually get scratched or cut at frequent intervals – when we had Fenella, the fox cub, she bit us all, affectionately but firmly, about once a week – and so we all have the routine three-yearly booster injections against tetanus.

One of the foals caught the horrible disease. It was a part-bred colt, an alert, well-built little creature which Dominie had bred to be a riding pony. The first indication of the disease was the sight of the colt standing in an oddly extended position with his muzzle stretched out before him and his tail raised behind: he strutted with an odd, stilt-like gait.

Mr Whippletree came to diagnose, and did so at a glance:

"Tetanus, probably caught it just after it was born, through the raw end of its umbilical cord touching the wet and muddy ground; this very rainy spring has caused a plague of the disease. He will become more and more rigid and eventually completely paralysed. This disease usually kills, particularly at this age, but we'll see what we can do. Keep it in conditions of the utmost quiet, for the ailment causes great agitation and mental distress. He will have to be injected with sedatives as well as anti-tetanus toxins. When the symptoms worsen you will have to force-feed the poor little thing."

As the disease progressed the colt grew stiffer and stiffer until he became as hard and as rigid as if he had been made of wood. Most of the time he lay on his side in the dark confines of a stable. When it was time for him to be fed and injected we would pick him up and set him on his feet as if he were a table, then push a tube behind his front teeth, which were clamped tight in a permanent seizure, and, once he was fed, lay him gently down on the straw again as if he were a piece of Chippendale furniture. For two weeks he had to be fed about every three hours. At night we would grumble out of bed, blear through the dark to his stable, fumblingly rub lanolin on to our frozen fingers, so as not to chafe the teats of his mother, milk her into a jug, feed the wretched little creature and then sleaze sleepily back to bed for a few more hours. Milking a mare is a tedious and unpleasant job: she has miserable little teats in comparison to a cow, is more restless and the milk is unpleasantly thick and sticky, like glue.

Gradually, the colt recovered, and it was with immense pleasure that Dominie, Mr Whippletree and I let him out again into the nursery pasture and saw his first tottering and convalescent hoof-steps as he staggered towards his foal friends, whinnying a weak greeting. They, being typical ponies, rushed up and gave him a thorough but cheerful pummelling for his absence.

Dominie began to need more help. She got plenty of advice and instruction, but not many people offered to join her in her daily undertaking of stable cleaning, swabbing the stable-yard, feeding, grooming and exercising the young stock, preparing for shows and organising visits from vet, farrier or customers. She did all this in addition to the routine of looking after a house, children, a husband and pets.

Beth was therefore taken into employment. She had just left school when she started with us: a small, pink-faced blonde who was an energetic and enthusiastic assistant when involved with the maintenance and handling of the ponies, but at first deeply embarrassed when involved with their sex life.

Eventually she became blasé, and I remember well the fastidious astonishment of one of the new work-experience girls as Beth told her what her duties were, meanwhile holding a cigarette in one hand and a busily servicing stallion in the other.

We have employed over a dozen work-experience girls. Dominie has taken their association with us very seriously and has done her utmost to find them jobs when their six months with us was over. Nearly all have been cheery and pleasant people to have around, although, to start with, some were naïvely ignorant of the work involved (two girls turned up in high heels for their first day); others were surprisingly puny (a hay-bale only weighs about four stone yet a few of the girls were unable to budge one). After their months with us were over, they had all developed beefy muscles and bossy voices.

Hay-making is the most testing and body-building of the jobs they have to do. To many people the haysel is a season of romance, percolated by the sweet smell of newly-cut grass and redolent of the images of horse and tumbril drifting over the heat-hazed fields whilst gaitered lads and low-bodiced lassies romp in the cosy confines of a hay-stack. This is not so. Firstly, hay-stacks always seem full of thistles. Secondly, Hart says that the haysel has always been known as the most energetic and tiring of all harvests. In the days of his youth it involved scything, raking and turning, raking again, stacking into small ricks, loading, transporting and unloading, stacking and thatching; now that it is all mechanised it consists of loading bales on to the tractor-trailer and unloading them into the barns. This normally takes place in June when, in theory, the weather is sunny, but theory does not always conform to fact and we often have to hurry and load our harvest, which averages 1,600 bales, about forty tons, before the Ascot-inspired rains start to fall.

Hay-making is, literally, a ticklish business, and because of this we got many volunteers. I could not understand why even my lazier friends, and once a whole platoon of soldiers from Colchester Garrison, offered to help. The only payment I gave was unlimited bottles of Mr Cook's good beer and plenty of fresh air. The real motivation dawned on me one day when Jennie walked past.

Jennie was employed by us after Beth left to get married. By that time Dominie was not only concentrating on breeding ponies, she was also beginning to sell some which had been broken in for riding or driving. Jennie had all the qualifications to help as she was an "AI", an Assistant Instructress, which meant that she had reached the standards set by the British Horse Society for teaching riding and managing equines. Jennie and her horse, T-Shirt, stayed with us for eight years, until she also left to get married, much to the disappointment of the local males, who liked her clothing during the hay-making season: it consisted merely of bra, jeans, thigh boots and gloves. Dai Plimsoles used to set up his frantic jogging on the spot every time he saw her thus clothed. It must have been inconvenient for Jennie to be bared to the elements, but at least it brought in additional help.

Hay alone is not really good enough for high quality animals during the cold months, and brood mares need special foods when pregnant or suckling: thus the products of Mr Fleame, the miller, were put to use. His large and cheerful family have been millers locally for over a dozen generations, the stump of his ancestor's old windmill still stands in his yard, but he mills by electricity nowadays. The mill is an ideal mixture of peace and bustle: family

. . . . Jennie had all the qualifications . . .

houses line one side of the yard, roses and clematis climb their clapboarded walls, pigeons coo on the roof, an idle and corpulent cat shuns its task of pest control and snoozes in the "pending" tray in the brass and mahogany office; the rumble of rollers and grindstones can be heard within the main building, lorries and vans come and go, white-dusted figures climb up and down the outside stairs, bearing laden sacks.

There are as many contrasts inside the mill as outside: they mill by all three conventional methods – stones, rollers and hammer mills. The stones are used only for a select trade to "natural" food faddists who like to grind down their teeth on unrefined goodnesses such as mill-stone grit, haulms, husks and weed seeds. The rest of the machinery makes, amongst other things, some of the pony food, and Mr Fleame took me round his mill and explained the properties of each type of food.

"Firstly," he said, "you have the famous old standby of horses and Scotchmen, oats. Its main purpose is to give fibre and protein and 'pep'; too much can overheat and overanimate a horse – and Scotchmen, perhaps – that is why your wife uses it only to bolster up the less substantial members of her herd: foals during their first winter, and any brood mares which may temporarily become ill. All your animals are in prime condition, so we only lightly bruise our oats through our rollers for them, which splits the hard casing and makes them more digestible, but old horses with bad teeth need their oats crushed to make them more easily taken in. They don't like those so much, though; horses like the crunchiness of uncrushed oats.

"Bran is the other vital food your wife buys. It is made from wheat. The wheat berry "– I was intrigued by his use of the latter word –" has seven skins. When we put it through our rollers the wheatgerm and flesh is forced out and the flattened remnants which comprise the skins are sold as broad bran. This gives bulk and fibre to any food mixture and also acts as a gentle purge."

He paused to put his cat out of the "pending" tray into his "out" tray and took a bill out of the former. "Now here is an account from a supplier of flaked maize and barley. I do not have the equipment to process all the different types of food that I supply. In certain cases I have to sub-contract what my customers want to other processors. For maize and barley to be flaked, my supplier has a cooker about eighteen feet high. This cooking alters the

properties of the food, creating starch and sugars, in much the
same way as the heating action of an oast house affects malting
barley. Both these foods are fatteners, maize particularly; I understand that your wife only feeds it to her part-breds and riding
animals. The Welsh Mountain Ponies can take on enough fat and
muscle without this extra booster.

"The other things which we do not process in our own mill,
but for which we are responsible, are certain blended feeds, the
two most important of these for your stud farm are sugar beet,
which we have blended with molasses, and which your ponies eat
as a fattener and for bulk, and pony nuts, which are pellets
of compressed ingredients from our own recipe which includes
lucerne, cereals, soya beans and other proteins. Many millers
include hay, but not us. Pony nuts ought to be 'a meal in one', so
we are extra careful on quality control on these."

Dominie also buys linseed from Mr Fleame. This she soaks for
24 hours and then puts into the Aga overnight to cook. The
resulting gluey mass is doted upon by the animals and is a great
conditioner, giving them glossy coats and complacent expressions.
She buys vitamin blends from a few travelling salesmen: these
powders probably do a lot of good, but, in my opinion, are
virulent in both price and colouring.

CHAPTER 4

New Neighbours: Man and Beast

He was an hairy man, and girt
with a girdle of leather about his loins.
II Kings 1 viii

He took his name from his beard, but it was not the magnificent
fiery bush which the application "Rufus" suggests, it was a pitiful,
sparse little ginger tuft which looked as if it had been transplanted
from the armpit of a spider monkey. It waggled, goat-like, when
he spoke, a trait made more evident by his custom of shaving his
upper lip and thus isolating the beard upon the featureless plain of
his pinched, narrow face.

The thing which annoyed most of us about Rufus was not that
he had so many mistresses, but that they were so pretty. It was
unnatural and illogical, we agreed, that this weedy and futile
ex-schoolmaster, staring resentfully at the world through thick
spectacles, selfish, bigoted and pedantic, should have three such
good-looking paramours. He was interesting, of course, for he
was a continuous source of obscure knowledge, but even then he
annoyed, for he was inclined to lecture his acquaintances with
patronising condescension.

Nevertheless, he became our friend.

I do not think one can choose a friend, friendships happen, one
suddenly realises that a person is likeable for his faults as well as
his virtues: Rufus, Millicent, Gloria and Karen; Hippocampus,
The August-Personage-In-Jade, Nibbles and Frodo – they all

became our close friends for over a year until an unfortunately misinterpreted message from God resulted in a stretch in Chelmsford Prison for Rufus and the break-up of the rest of their small community.

We met them first one cold February day when the dreary grey skies wept a thin mizzle into my garden and the snowdrops and winter aconites trembled in the blustery wind. We were all assembled in the kitchen for elevenses: Tony Crisp and Mr Ryan steaming in front of the stove and Monk lecturing Bradawl and Hart on the reasons why Colchester United, although a better and more pleasing team than Ipswich, was not yet as successful. A timid knock on the door was barely heard. I bellowed, "Come in," above the hubbub and a wispy-looking wraith of a girl entered. She was tall and thin and bony, her height emphasised by long pale hair which streamed down to her waist, by pendant loops of necklaces made from wooden beads, nuts, berries and shells which reached her belt and by a heavy corduroy maxi-skirt which swept the floor. She had huge, blank, sky-blue eyes and a pretty pointed face like that of an absent-minded elf.

"Peace Be With You," she murmured in a low and earnest voice.

We gazed back at her with mild unease, nonplussed by her soppy greeting.

"Our Horse has cast a Shoe, can we have Permission to pitch on your Land till we have him re-shod?"

"You're in luck," said Dominie. "The farrier is coming round to shoe a pony this afternoon; you can put your caravan in the paddock at the end of the garden: your horse can graze there and there's a tap at the corner of the field."

"Crumbs!" said Candy in a long, wavering wail of delight as she, Mr Dewbit and I saw the caravan which stood in the paddock. It was a beautifully painted and carved gypsy waggon of the type I later learned was called a Burton. It was about fourteen feet long and towered high above its wheels, the front pair being slightly smaller than the rear; the match-boarded walls were reinforced by balustrades of carved ribs; also carved and scalloped were the weather-boards which edged the curved roof; there was a window each side, with little shutters; at the back there was another small window and a large pan-box slung between the rear wheels; in front there was a wide, high driving platform and the entrance, a double door, glazed on its upper half. The general colour scheme was red and yellow; the suit of harness, which hung from a hook near the door, was mainly black with red trimming and was a-glitter with metal work.

A curved flight of steps had been hung on to the driving platform between the lowered shafts, and two women ornamented it. The one we had already met stood up from the lower step and came towards us. She was holding a large bundle of chestnut-coloured fur: its emission of malevolent growls disclosed that it was a Pekinese.

"Peace Be With You," she said.

We muttered sheepishly in return.

She indicated the Pekinese: "The August-Personage-In-Jade."

The August-Personage started at the sound of his name, looked angrily about and snarled, no messages of peace from him.

A fine, well-groomed skewbald cob grazed a few paces off.

"Hippocampus," she said. Hippocampus raised a large, Roman-nosed head, glanced benevolently at us, and then continued grazing.

The other girl came up to us. She had high cheek-bones and a heart-shaped face framed by glossy brown curls: she looked a bit like Vivien Leigh.

"My Sister-in-Love, Gloria."

Gloria smiled back and said in broadest Cockney: "'Allo, luvs."

"And I am Millicent. Come, let us Proceed together and meet the rest of the Family-in-Spirit."

So up the ladder we went, through the door, bowing to avoid the hanging cage of Frodo, a canary, and into the snug shadows of the caravan. The first impression was of scent, a mixture of wood smoke, furniture polish and sandalwood, the second impression was of the warmth, radiating from a small, rectangular stove in a tiled alcove on our left. The interior was immaculately neat: the shelves were dust-free and tidily stacked with rows of books, utensils and ornaments; the brass of the gas-lamps glowed; frilly chintz curtains swathed each tiny window; from hooks, crockery and cooking equipment hung, arranged in order of size; the fitted furniture gleamed. A pair of bunk beds took up the whole width of the caravan at the rear, the lower bed looked crisp and clean, with fluffy blankets and white linen, the hems of the pillows and the sheet turn-over beautifully embroidered with garlands of wild flowers. The only scruffy item lay on the upper bed comprising a weedy pair of legs in darned jeans, a check shirt open to show a scattering of freckles and ginger hairs on a narrow chest and a long, thin neck about the same circumference and colour as an old land-drain and festooned with leather strings and metal chains from which dangled Egyptian amulets, CND badges, a small brass "piskey", Thor hammers and other archaic cult symbols. A pair of spectacles glittered towards us as we approached and a languid hand was fluttered. "Greetings, friends," boomed a deep voice.

At his feet the third girl sat. Like the others she was in her early twenties: her blonde hair was plaited into painful-looking rat-tails threaded through with beads and she was dressed entirely in plum-coloured velvet, except for a white-ruffled blouse cut low to reveal a large pair of bosoms, between which Mr Dewbit and I involuntarily peered. Karen, for such was her name, lilted a greeting in a Norwegian accent and we all went to inspect the horse.

Mr Dewbit looked pensive and then shook his head: "This sometimes happens to heavy horses if they do a lot of road work, he's starting to get ringbone – a growth of extra bone on the pastern."

Millicent set up a keening lament.

"There may be no need to worry, it could be a non-articular, which means that it will cure after a long rest; whatever it is, you'll need the vet, and you'll have to stay here for some time, or get a new horse if you want to go far."

Rufus looked glum and futile. Gloria turned to me.

"'Ave you got anywhere where we can stay?"

"Well . . ." I said doubtfully.

"Daddy," hissed Candy, "pleeeeeeease!"

And so it was that the little community encamped in half an acre of rough gound next to Bell Pit Wood, a couple of fields away from our house. Their camp was by a small rill which gave them water for ordinary use; drinking water was drawn off from the pipe in the next field which supplied some pony drinking troughs. I gave Rufus the right of "estovers" for their stay, which meant that they could gather any fallen or dead timber – but not any green or growing wood. Mr Whippletree diagnosed Hippocampus' problem as the less-virulent non-articular lameness and said that when the callouses had completely formed the lameness would go and be unlikely to return if they limited their daily journeys. Hippocampus grazed the half acre, it was not a very good pasture as it had recently been cleared of a crop of young Christmas trees, but as he was not at work he had no need to be too fussy about his food. Gloria, who acted as chief spokesman, asked me if they could stay for six months, for Mr Whippletree had told them that Hippocampus needed at least four months free from labour; if I allowed them a couple of extra months they would be able to plant and harvest some potatoes and vegetables. This horrified Monk, who became convinced that they would nourish themselves entirely on his pheasants, and it disgusted most of the others, who thought them immoral. Candy was delighted and visited them often, returning home garlanded with daisy chains and a-babble with stories about the travelling people and furry and feathered friends. The little commune, especially Millicent, took particularly fondly to Candy: I think that perhaps they regretted having no children, "Though it's not for want of trying, I'll be bound," said Hart darkly and Monk nodded in agreement. "I can hardly hear myself think when I'm doing the night rounds in Bell Pit Wood, because of the panting and snorting coming from that caravan."

I had been asked to submit receipts for a cookery book being published to earn money for the Distressed Gentlefolks Association: all the receipts were to be given by men and, if possible, had to be original or unusual. We also had to cook each receipt ourselves, to ascertain the time spent in cooking and preparation. I know little about cooking, though I did make quite a good soup once out of the only things I found in my parents' London flat – a tin of tunny fish, some ginger biscuits and three bottles of tomato juice – so I was forced to look for inspiration. Monk, who had been reared in the marshlands, gave me a receipt for samphire, Bradawl told me about a Christmas punch (it was almost neat whisky, with a dash of brandy and hot water and a sprinkle of sugar and nutmeg. Even the fumes from the earthenware jug it seethed in sent Mrs Pipkin into a tizzy of alcoholic merriment), and Hart told me about vermin stew. Basically, it is a concoction of the animals that the villagers were allowed to trap and eat on the estate when he was a boy – rabbits, pigeons and sparrows. I tried it out, with a few suggestions and additions from Dominie, and it is quite delicious, but it took me two hours to prepare and another three to cook.

George, Charlie, Monk and I went out one day to gather the main ingredients. George lurked, gun in hand, in a ditch by a field of oil-seed rape: Monk set out some plastic decoy pigeons, gave him some small forked twigs to use to prop up any other pigeons that he shot and wanted to use as extra decoys and reminded him to set them up-wind as that was the direction that the birds would face when alighting and feeding. Charlie went off to a field of spring barley to empty the sparrow traps, with strict instructions to release any birds which were not sparrows. Monk and I went to a warren in a bank between Fenn Field and Coppin's Wood. Monk netted all the burrows but two, down one of which he put Captain Farqueson the XXIInd; I shot the rabbits as they escaped from the other; Monk supervised the nets. When eight furry corpses were hanging from his carry-stick by their threaded-through back legs and the ferret had emerged from the excavated warren, we returned to find the boys. Monk took the seven brace that George had shot, and the thirty-two brace of sparrows, and went home with them to prepare them for the pot; the boys and I walked back to Wastewood through the twilight. The scene was idyllic as we approached the encampment. Hippocampus was grazing peacefully by the little brook, The August-Personage-In-Jade and Gloria were lying on the sward beside a small bonfire over which a cauldron hung, its bubbling just audible between the pauses of Frodo's song as he carolled in melodious competition against a blackbird in an adjacent thorn thicket; Millicent, sitting on the lowest step of the entrance ladder, was embroidering and repeating responses to the psalm-like chants of Rufus, who sat cross-legged at her feet, his eyes closed and his hands hovering over a pile of seed potatoes before him. Karen was digging in a fenced-off area.

Rufus, who knew we were there, and knew that we knew he knew we were there, continued to chant for a minute or so but finally condescended to open his eyes and speak to us.

"I am uttering benison upon the food-children that we plant, that they may come forth bountifully, and that they may forgive us, as the worm forgives the plough, when their time comes to become as one with our mortal flesh."

"Affected twit," I thought, but aloud I said, offering a brace of rabbits, "We don't need all we got today, would you like these?"

Millicent gave a faint little cry and gazed at us with huge reproachful eyes. "Oh, the Poor, Dear Lost Ones; how Could you? What would your God say?"

"My God made me omnivorous, in the same way as he made your horse herbivorous and your Pekinese, from what I've seen of him, extremely carnivorous."

Rufus hastily interrupted, he knew that although Millicent and I could tolerate each other, after more than a minute together we became extremely irritated. "Although Millicent is quite rightly a vegetarian, I am obliged to eat meat as I need the extra energy it gives me in order to keep up my strength for my duties."

"Good," I replied. "You know that you offered to do some work for me as rent for this site? Well, I'd now like to take up your offer."

His jaw dropped, his eyes went glassy; he looked as aghast as if Hippocampus had strolled over and suddenly hoofed him in the solar plexus.

"I want you to do daily check-ups on the fencing for my wife's ponies and for some sheep which we've just been offered."

The sheep were unexpected additions to the family.

In front of an old stone house in one of the outer islands of the Kingdom of Scotland, so far north that it is as close to the Arctic Circle as it is to the borders with England, a small, ramshackle van was being loaded beneath the cold clouds of dawn. First to go in were three lobsters, snugly packed in a cardboard box lined with damp seaweed, their nippers tied with twine; next to enter were three Shetland sheep, Baabaara, who was white, Bathshebaa, who was gold, and Maagnus, who was black; they were followed by Moss, a sheep-dog with a wonkey kneecap; finally, two people, a man and his wife, squeezed in. About 24 hours and 800 miles later the van drew up outside our front door. We peered through the steamed-up windows, 18 eyes of different sizes and colours gazed groggily back, various odd shapes and objects loomed through the fug: horns, hooves, heads, paws, pincers, hair, wool, teeth and fangs. I opened the door and a rancid mist billowed out: the result of a day and night of chain-smoking humans, sea-sicking dog, excrementing and urinating sheep and slobbering lobsters.

Within a very short time, the lobsters had been boiled and eaten; Moss, the dog, had had his knee-cap filed into shape by Mr Whippletree; Robert and Caroline had completed their annual cultural orgy in London (the opera, the ballet, the latest films, the theatre, art galleries, a ride on the top of a bus and a visit to the monkey-house in the zoo); and the three sheep had been put out to graze. That's how we started sheep farming.

"She is her own worst enemy," said someone of a film star to Groucho Marx.

"Not while I'm alive, she's not," he replied.

So it is also that "the worst enemy of a sheep is another sheep", spreading diseases to each other and leading one another astray, but having often chased escaped sheep over several hundred acres of heavy ploughland I would willingly take their place as their chief enemy.

Great Britain contains more sheep per acre than any other nation, except New Zealand. We have been famous for our sheep for almost two and a half millennia. During the Middle Ages wool was our most significant export: evidence of its importance being the "Woolsack", still the official seat of the Lord Chancellor in the House of Lords, and in the beautiful "wool churches", mostly in the Perpendicular style of the fifteenth century, such as Long Melford, Lavenham and Thaxted. Centuries of breeding have divided our sheep into almost forty different types, specialists for two end-uses, meat or wool; the wool itself is divided up into categories, ranging from the coarse "carpet yarn" wool of the Lincolns, Leicesters and Cheviots to the finer wools of those such as of the Oxford Downs, Dorset Horns and Ryelands. However, we rarely keep sheep for milking, as they do in Europe and particularly in France. I used to watch my cousin's flocks in the Massif Central being rounded up each evening for milking time: the milk would be made into Roquefort cheese.

Our local sheep are Suffolk Blackfaces: they have no horns, their dense fleece is of high quality and they make good mutton.

Our Shetlanders, like most animals from those islands, are smaller than average and very hardy, being able to live on a meagre diet of seaweed, heather and coarse grass. Their most remarkable difference from nearly all other sheep is their moulting: they do not have to be shorn, their fleece peels away in scruffy patches during spring and can be "wool-gathered" from the ground and off the prickles and thorns of scrub. Like gleaning, wool-gathering used to be a right in parts of Britain, but apart from the Shetlanders most sheep contribute only a little to the poor of a parish in this way.

I became intrigued by all the different rights and asked Cedric Cattermole, the estate agent, to send me a list of the basic rights the parishioners may be allowed over an estate. Cattermole sent me the following list:

Rights of Pasture	(grazing, also "cattle gates")
Rights of Pannage	(pigs after acorns, etc.)
Rights of Turbary	(gathering of peat as fuel)
Rights of Estovers	(wood fallen off trees)
Rights of Bruary	(cutting bracken)
Rights of Piscary	(fishing)
Rights of Gleaning	(gathering corn left by reapers)
Rights of Common in the soil	(the taking of sand, gravel, stones, clay, coal or water)

As we did not have any adequately fenced-in grazing, our three sheep went to live temporarily with the Ropers, who had paddocked a field next to their garden for some Jacobs and Saint Kildas. Maagnus did not particularly mind the Jacobs, idle animals with blotched, piebald markings, but for some reason the Saint Kildas infuriated him. They were small, svelte, black creatures with long, slim legs and beret-like bobbles between their ears; the ewes looked rather like Marlene Dietrich, but what riled Maagnus was Stanley, the ram, who had four magnificent horns, two curling over his ears and two like prongs, jutting out from his forehead. Maagnus' insignificant little curlicues looked pathetic beside Stanley's colossal armoury, and Maagnus knew it. He therefore picked several fights, like a football fan whose team has just lost, and was soundly beaten each time. He then re-directed his energies and decided that the most interesting and amusing thing to do was to escape from his enclosure: he jumped over the post-and-rails, he wriggled under the wires, he opened gate latches and he squeezed through slats. The Ropers became thoroughly annoyed with kindly telephone calls from neighbours saying, "Sorry to ring you at five in the morning, but one of your sheep has woken us up by baa-ing outside our window."

Finally, in a rage, I plonked Maagnus into the front seat of our tatty little Mini (which I had bought from Mr Ryan for £60) and drove a couple of miles to the nearest slaughterhouse. When we arrived a group of gossiping men turned from their chatter to look at us and, seeing Maagnus sitting on the seat next to me staring worriedly through the windscreen, they emitted prolonged cheers and applause.

The head knacker was beefy and blood-stained, he stuck his head through our window.

. . . . staring worriedly through the windscreen . . .

"How much will you charge to slaughter and joint him?" I hissed in a tactful aside.

He prodded the glum-looking sheep with callous, callused fingers.

"Nice and fat," he said. "Three quid if I can keep the pelt."

Next time I saw poor Maagnus, he was in twelve plastic bags.

He was particularly delicious when roasted.

A year later Robert arrived with Stephen and Matilda so I relieved the Ropers of their tedious tenants and put all the sheep in a rough part of my parents' garden, where they mowed and fertilised the grass so efficiently that I later suggested, during a district council meeting, that not only could we save £80,000 per year on maintenance by releasing sheep in the graveyards under the care of the council, but we could actually make a profit. The idea was greeted with cries of indignation from my brother councillors and a snide editorial from a local paper.

Stephen also paid a short and fatal visit to the local knacker; he was what is known as "a sexual deviationist", utterly ignoring the woolly charms of his wives and moping after the sleeker outlines of Cymbeline's Galewarning, who was not only a pony, but a male pony. His place was taken by a hearty and completely heterosexual Suffolk ram called BG 14: the resulting lambs have the fine fleece and superb mutton of their dams with the docility, weight and good health of their sire.

There was a roar of repressed thunder. The huge body rose from its pad in a billow of smoke and flame, hovered for a few brief moments, then turned its colossal bulk on its axis. The blunted nose reared up and pointed to the Galaxy of Thoth, wherein lived the Grutelwigz, the tentacled beings of the planet Cyberus. With a final roar the Spacesearcher vanished into the inky depths of space.

So it was that the Spacesearcher set off on her journey when the thumb of Alexus Borth, her captain, had pressed her starter button, and so it was when the wet nose of Potter, my black labrador, touched the electric fence which confined my sheep to their pasture.

Fencing is a vexed question, the vexation being caused by the terrible expense. The most attractive and effective fencing I have seen has been in the fat pastures of Sussex, oaken post and rails which retained the sleek and pampered presences of racehorses; the cheapest "fencing" I have seen was a small Arab boy on a donkey trying to contain a flock of Nubian goats and being paid a handful of dates per day for his labours. No livestock is safe with barbed wire and the herdsmen of valuable beasts will not use it; electric fencing is easy to use and reasonably cheap as it can be transported from field to field, but it can cause a mental "frisson" to an animal: a pony which has been electrified several times may become uneasy and nervy. Because of the great expense of fencing I decided to re-work some of the old chestnut coppicing in Hadrian's Wood. This had not been harvested since the 1950s, and the stools had sprouted growths which were now as thick as telegraph poles, very difficult to split into post-sized widths. I eventually found that it was preferable to saw the wood up into logs, which could then be sold to some of the many people who had succumbed to the fad for log-burning stoves for their central heating, and with the money I could buy some decent fencing. After ten years, the coppiced areas are now looking as if they will produce suitable fencing timber, and the ground beneath has sprouted with the growth which had become swamped and obscured by the dense shade of the untilled chestnuts: primroses, wood anemone, enchanter's nightshade, bugle, ground ivy, foxglove and creeping Jennie.

Having been given the sheep and having found a way of paying for at least part of the fencing, I thought it would be convenient to rear ponies and sheep together. I thought I might make a lot of money out of the sheep themselves, their wool and the huge subsidies I imagined the Common Market would pay me; I thought that Dominie, who dotes on all animals, would become entranced and so concentrate on these potential moneymakers that she would cut down on the numbers of ponies and I would get my money back in a couple of years.

I was wrong.

I discovered that, although it can sometimes be advantageous to rear ponies and sheep together since, like cows and ponies, they destroy each other's parasites, the former combination is not nearly so effective as the latter. The sheep-grazing technique is similar to that of equines – they are nibblers – added to which, some ponies and horses enjoy chasing sheep, a sport particularly bad for the latter during lambing. And worst of all, Dominie thought that the sheep had silly voices and faces. Finally, like any new business, the only person who seems to be a beneficiary is the money-lender. Cedric Cattermole, the suavely efficient estate agent, produced some pessimistic statistics. The minimum viable sheep "station" would be of 120 acres holding 600 breeding sheep. It would cost £40,000 to buy stock, £10,000 to prepare the land (fencing, sowing, etc.), and another £10,000 for equipment; having thus borrowed £60,000 from the bank I would then have to spend about another £15,000 per year, this included a variety of costs of which the greatest proportion would be the shepherd's wages. Sales would be around £40,000 per year.

I therefore decided to be my own shepherd, and to let my flock grow and become profitable by degrees, letting the numbers propagate through natural increase, selling the wether (castrated male) lambs and keeping the gimmer (female) lambs and culling the ill or barren ewes. Thus, in theory, our primary stock of ten sheep could multiply to a viable number, assuming that most of the ewes had twins and that half were female.

We have not yet succeeded. Rufus was hopeless at his job of fence-master, he only did it for a week and then told Karen to take over. A gang of rustlers stole several sheep one night, killer dogs have harassed lambs and the Shetlands sometimes find our vegetation too rich and unhealthy for their digestions. However, we are now building up the numbers, I like them, and Dominie has a multi-coloured shawl spun and woven from our wool by Millicent. Dominie says she will wear it when she is a hundred and finally looks like "Granny Buggins", whoever she may be.

CHAPTER 5

Buying and Selling

An ass's head was sold for four score
pieces of silver, and the fourth part of
a kab of dove's dung for five pieces of silver.
II Kings 6 xxv

We slithered up a deeply rutted drive, pock-marked with pot-holes; some of the larger had been filled in with broken bricks or rubble so that Mr Ryan cursed and mourned for his tyres as his van juddered and slewed through them. An appalling stench grasped us by the sinuses and made our eyes water; the dead trees on either side of the drive must have died through pollution rather than Dutch Elm disease. The ditch on my side was full of thick green liquor, upon which clots and scabs floated; the verge to our right was sprinkled with assorted litter ranging from empty plastic sacks and old tractor tyres, to rusted oil drums and the guts of machines; most of this was half hidden by patches of nettle or clumps of bramble.

Eventually we saw a group of sway-backed shacks, sheds and hovels. Their roofs, although varied in covering – asbestos sheets, pantiles, corrugated iron, slates or rotten thatch – were united in their ramshackle and holed condition.

The farmhouse which dominated the clutter had once been pleasant. To a single Tudor hall with a steep-pitched roof and large chimneys a variety of out-houses and lean-tos had been added, some of them merging compatibly with the original building,

50

others showing their cheap-jack origins in the alien roof slate or the crumbling pebbledash coating.

All the buildings faced on to a yard, a sea of liquefied mud with the occasional island of a dungle rising from it. A few moulting chickens perched on them like refugees in a flood. They stood silent and dejected, the only noises were porcine squeals from a line of pigsties to our right, a weird, irregular grinding from an old wooden railway waggon beside us and intermittent growling from a barrel containing a chained cur of unknown breed.

Mr Ryan looked about him and kicked a dead rat pensively. "By God, I've heard that Essex is the 'county of filthy farmyards' but this always strikes me dumb with disgust."

He knocked on the blistered and leprously blotched paint that covered the back door which immediately swung open and a rancid smell of boiled cabbage and unwashed slovenliness wafted out. A grey-faced drab wearing a greasy pinafore stared peevishly at us.

"Watcher want?" she snapped.

"Is Mr Hardcroft in, me flower?" Ryan asked.

The slattern ran a wizened hand through her balding tresses and tittered in an arch and provocative manner.

"I know your sort, Michael Ryan!" she shouted, then, altering her voice into an eldritch screech, called, "Hebidiah!" over her shoulder.

Her husband loomed out of the squalid gloom of the kitchen. He was a huge, silent hulk overdressed in an assortment of clothes, mainly knitted and including two jerseys under a cardigan, a scarf and a pair of holed mittens from which peeked a clutch of vast, chilblained fingers like the teats of a nanny goat. He looked broodingly at our rubber boots, besmirched by our wade through the slops and puddles of his yard, and pointed to a bucket of fluid and a lopsided sign by the entrance gate. The sign said –

SLOUGHHOLLOW FARM
KEEP OUT, SWINE FEVER

"Did you disinfect your boots when you came in?" he asked.

"No, we didn't," replied Mr Ryan, "but we bloody well will when we leave."

Mr Hardcroft silently bent over, his face went scarlet and he emitted a collection of wheezings which changed into a hacking cough.

He had laughed.

Mr Ryan then introduced me and said that we had come to see the colt he had for sale. Whilst he spoke, an infant of vile appearance came up and stared at us. Its face was almost entirely covered with the stickier sorts of food: jam, chocolate and crumbs of something I hoped were only cake in its hair. Its index finger was plunged almost up to the knuckle in a nostril.

"Shake hands with Mr Courtauld," urged its proud mother.

Please God, don't let it, I silently prayed.

It stared at me in sullen silence, its finger-tip still probing.

"Go on, shake hands."

Please God, yeugh!

"Gladwin, Mr Courtauld wants to shake hands!"

Gladwin and I continued to stare at each other. The brat finally extracted its finger but, to my relief, instead of offering me its repulsive hand it spoke:

"The nasty gentleman's got a cross face," it noted shrewdly, and then began to bawl.

The child was swept back into the kitchen by its fussing mother and its father took us over to the goods waggon, unbolted the door and flung it open.

The cause of the grinding which we had heard on entering the yard became apparent. A miserable palomino stood in the semi-darkness and, not even bothering to look up on our entry, continued to gaze glassy-eyed at a wall whilst gnawing raspingly at its manger.

"It will be crib-biting next," said Mr Ryan with malicious satisfaction. "The poor creature is bored stiff." He turned to me and ignoring the increasingly lowering expression of Mr Hardcroft, continued: "You must look after an animal's mind as well as its body. Boredom is the worst problem, and you can usually tell that it's happening in three ways: wind-sucking and crib-biting, which are different ways of gulping in air, and weaving, when it sways from side to side without stopping. It is surprising that this poor little feller has had time to be bored, it's got saddle-girth sores, see the runny patches on its back and sides, poll evil, other runny sores at the top of its head, and either laminitis or seedy toe – I'll have to look closer to see what's causing it to limp."

He straightened up from his perusal of a hoof and gave a disparaging glance at the colt.

"What do you want for him?"

Mr Hardcroft scowled. "Apart from the saddle-sores, which he had when I bought him last week, there's nothing wrong with him and you know it. I've got a vet's certificate of health. £400."

Mr Ryan laughed heartily at this quaint price. "Tell you what," he suggested, "I'll take it in my horse-box to Trotters Rest, so that they can put it out of its misery, and if I can keep its hooves for glue I won't charge you the cost of transport."

"£400."

Mr Ryan sighed. "Look, those sores show it's been broken-in badly." He prised apart its lips and peered into its mouth. "Looks a bit parrot-mouthed to me – its top teeth overhang the lower ones," he said to me in a loud aside, "I'll give you £50 for it."

"Its teeth are perfect, £350."

"You know nothing about ponies, you are only interested in those great old Suffolk Punches of yours. I'll give you £100 to take it off your hands."

"I know any good bit of livestock when I see it, you know that, else you wouldn't be here, £300."

"£150."

"£280."

"£250, and that's my last."

"£250 – done," said Hardcroft: they slapped the palms of their hands together to confirm the offer.

The wretched animal would not box.

Mr Ryan led her up to the shack on wheels which served as his trailer; the pony shied away from it.

Mr Ryan walked in a circle, sloshing through the mud, and tried again. The pony dug its front hooves into the ground and leaned back, almost squatting. Mr Ryan sighed, organised the opening of the front door of the trailer, and approached the ramp at a trot. The pony slithered to a halt, and then reared up with its eyes starting and its ears flattened back.

Mrs Hardcroft, who had been watching these efforts, filled the lap of her pinafore with straw from a rotting stack and strewed it on the ramp for camouflage. The pony was deluded into walking a couple of steps in it, but when it heard the hollow drumming of its hooves beneath it, shied back and tried to bolt out of the yard.

Mr Ryan made the old mistake of hanging on when he had lost his balance. There was a massive PLOPP as he fell into the mire and then a sliding, splattering noise as he was towed towards the gate. There the pony stopped and Mr Ryan rose to his feet, wet, dark and shapeless like an enormous stewed prune. Although I could see he was mouthing comments I could not hear them because of the shrill screams of merriment from the crone and the hacking coughs from her spouse.

Mr Ryan, clothes and all, was hosed down. He grasped the pony's leading rein with stubborn determination. A bucket of crushed oats was temptingly flitted beneath the beast's nose. It remained as immobile as Stonehenge.

Mr Hardcroft said, "We'll haul the bugger in." An assortment of ropes were threaded through parts of the trailer and either tied to the animal's halter or passed round its behind: we all heaved, the animal was forced halfway up the ramp; it then fell over, snapping its crude halter as it did so.

When, at last, it was recaptured and led once more to the foot of the ramp, Mrs Hardcroft appeared with a stiff bristled broom.

"This often works, leastways it did with my grandfather, who was an ostler at The King's Head on the Great East Road." She then brushed the ground noisily behind the rear of the pony. The animal, disliking the sound and the occasional prod she gave him with the broomhead, scuttled up the ramp, Mrs Hardcroft sweeping furiously and loudly after him.

"Thank you, flower, I always knew you had a way with the boys," beamed Mr Ryan.

"Get on with you, you filthy dog," she screamed, gratified.

This was my first experience of horse coping, but that was before Dominie had started up her stud farm – the little palomino was for Mr Ryan's grandson – and it was Captain Firecrest who taught us the principles of "dealing". He refuses to use the word "coping" as it suggests sharp practice and no one is more honest than the Captain, although he is extemely subtle in his honesty.

"You must know two things: the mind of your opponent, and the true worth of the animal. A sale is a battle between two sides, trying to get the better of each other; if you want to win you must find out your opponent's weakest point, the minimum price he'll accept, and you must stop him finding out how high you are prepared to go; that's if you're buying. It's obviously the reverse if you're selling. And of course you must be able to assess the good and bad points of the animal very quickly."

The wind sweeping over the flat paddocks on the derelict aerodrome made the Captain's slight form sway on its heels as he stared at the stock being paraded in the sale ring. He is a grim-faced, wiry man with abrupt movements, "as gaunt as a greyhound and as busy as a bodylouse", said Hart said one day. He dresses more like a dealer in City stocks than in livestock: black suit, shiny shoes, regimental tie and bowler hat, only a cluster of Member's tickets about his umbrella handle betray his interests. As well as his suit, he also habitually wears an expression of utter dejection, gazing out into the world from a pair of rusty green eyes which stain his cadaverous face like mould patches on a coffin lid. He has a short temper with humans and a kind word – though a disparaging glance – for any horse or pony. When not at work he opens the handle of his umbrella, which transforms it into a shooting-stick and, sitting on it, reads a pocket bible. Most of the quotations at the head of the chapters in this book were learned from him.

Pamela Rantipole had introduced him to Dominie and had suggested that we hire him one day to act as buyer and negotiator on our behalf.

"He's a gloomy sort of chap, but he'll be worth the money; he's a good teacher, has terrific flair for a bargain and can show you the basic problems and methods of buying and selling."

Dominie had bought a horse magazine and read some of the advertisements and descriptions as we drove to the aerodrome in Captain Firecrest's ancient but immaculate Jaguar.

"11.3 hands. Grey mare, young; a good ride for a strong child; could be used for stud or in a good home."

"Don't touch that with a barge pole," said the Captain. "'Young' can mean anything; reading between the lines it suggests that the pony is difficult to control, is a puller and that they want to see the end of it; they don't say things like it being good in traffic, if it's sound or easy to box. You can often read more from what is left out than from what is put in."

When buying a pony for stud work, Dominie has two options, either "form" or "blood lines". "Form" means that the animal has won in the show-ring, the quality of the shows being more important than the quantity; from its record one should be able to judge how good it is. "Form" can be expensive, "blood lines", on the other hand, can sometimes be cheap, and one can find that the only other bidder for a horse of blood line at an auction is the dog-meat man. Good blood lines have their own well-known characteristics: for example, some may produce a certain shaped head, or a good action when trotting, or a good temperament or high withers; by blending alternative characteristics a good breeder should be able to make exactly "the right pudding from the ingredients". Dominie told Captain Firecrest that she was interested in brood mares whose blood lines were known for their good conformation but also, of even more importance to her, for their excellent temperaments. She had decided that the Cymbeline Stud ponies should become known not only for their good looks, but also for their gentle and agreeable natures.

As we sat in the traffic jam before the aerodrome, the Captain explained his basic policies and methods.

"'Buy at a market, but sell at home', that's my motto. You usually find better prices at an auction and you can see the animal at its worst: in crowded conditions, being harassed, with noise and traffic and other animals around it. At home it will be at ease in familiar surroundings, well-groomed, and my nagsman can show it to its best advantage over the flat or jumps. Of course, if you don't know much about the subject, you are better off buying from a reputable person at home, you'll be able to try out the animal, which you certainly can't do with one at an auction. I'll see if I can negotiate a sale before the animal gets registered for the auction. When I am talking to a seller, please keep silent, 'a closed mouth suggests a wise head', I always say."

The sale was slightly unusual in that some stock was being offered away from the auction rings. In most auctions, stock has to be registered before the catalogue is printed or, at latest, once the horse has entered the car-park. As we walked down the lines of stock for sale the Captain kept up a low-voiced running commentary, pausing occasionally to lift his hat gravely to an acquaintance or to detour fastidiously a puddle or heap of dung.

"First we look for obvious faults. If there are any objectionable ones we look no further. Then we look for good points; 'buyers want a hundred eyes, sellers none', I always say. Any sign of vice should condemn an animal at once, however good its conformation. Look at this horse with a bulging forehead, the 'mad bump' we call it – it is often a sign of viciousness; the animal is black as well which I think the most beautiful of all colours for a horse, but I rarely suggest blacks or chestnuts to novice riders, they can have bad temperaments."

His ears pricked and his eyes brightened as he noticed something else to be disparaging about. "Hear that? 'A dry cough is the trumpeting of death.'"

We continued to walk down the lines. The Captain nattered on: "Too weedy . . . blue eyes, not often liked . . . touch of laminitis . . . been fired, maybe all right . . . had lice . . . skewbald, gypsy's pony . . . saw her sold at another sale last month, must be something wrong . . . 'you can tell a horse by his harness', see, a broken and dirty head collar, badly mended, must have been slovenly kept, may have broken the collar in a struggle, may not like being boxed, quiet enough now, too quiet, may be sedated . . . ah, here we are at the first of your mares, not bad at first sight."

We had stopped by an affable-looking grey Welsh Mountain Pony who had thrust her muzzle into the contents of a hay-net. She raised an eyebrow to look at us, and then continued to munch while the Captain went on lecturing:

"Now, I divide my judgements into seven groups, which I always take in the same order.

"Firstly, mental condition: she has no apparent stable or psychological vices, does not object to humans – no ears back, no whites of eyes showing nor swinging round to kick; well-tempered; seems intelligent and alert; quiet, not nervy or jumpy; kind, perhaps a bit pert, but no harm in that.

"Second, a brief look at physical health: bright eyes, good shiny coat, eating well; no visible outer signs of ill-health, I'll know better when she is run out. It can take time to know if an animal is completely healthy: under the laws of Howell the Good, the Prince of Wales about a thousand years ago, a buyer was allowed three set periods to ensure that his purchase was free of three special diseases: three nights for the staggers, three months for any lung problem and one year for infestation of glanders.

"Third, I look for its age. You can tell an animal's age by looking at its teeth; their state of growth and wear are pretty accurate as indicators up to nine years, though they can be forged with filing and pulling, and at a later age you can tell by the colour of the teeth, the thickness of the tartar and their angle of projection; now, the advertisement said she was four, she should have fully-

developed central nippers, slightly blunted, the next pair will be
up but small with a deep mark that extends right across . . ."

His voice became muffled as he peered further down the mare's
throat. He re-surfaced.

"Yes, she's four. Incidentally, other signs of old age include
grey hairs, hollows over the eyes, a sunken back, sharp withers
and thin, hanging lips." I looked at him and hastily looked away,
embarrassed.

"Fourth, I look for 'presence' which combines the outward signs
of personality together with the general physical appearance and
carriage: how it holds itself. She looks lively and alert, quite pleased
with herself; good symmetrical body, well-balanced, won't breed
trippers or stumblers: skeleton and framework look sound; body
and limbs in the right proportions and set at the correct angles.

"Fifth, I look at the animal in more detail. A vet's certificate of
health is necessary if you are spending a lot on a really expensive
horse, but as it will cost you £50 you should trust your own
judgement as much as possible. I start by looking at the head and
neck; then the shoulder, forelegs and feet; back, loins and body;
lastly the quarters, hind legs and feet."

He then proceeded to inspect the pony from nostril to tail tip,
rattling off comments for our benefit: "Clear nose – bright eyes –
nice little dished face – alert expression – neat little ears . . ." at
which point the owner came up, an anxious-looking woman in a
heavy hairnet and with thighs so large that they ballooned her
jodhpurs out like an ostrich's drumsticks. The Captain worked his
way down the pony under the increasingly apprehensive gaze of
its owner. His lifted eyebrow was occasionally raised in silent
criticism, he glanced up to heaven in speechless supplication a
couple of times and once allowed a sharp intake of breath to denote
shocked surprise. When he finally stepped away from the pony it
continued to look placid but its owner was scarlet and shiny with
agitation.

"Well, it is still alive," he commented non-committally. "Let's
see it in action, the sixth thing I look for."

The wretched woman untied the animal and began panting up
and down the sward beside it.

"She's got the technique," said the Captain approvingly. "In
comparison to her lumbering gait even an old crock would look
as graceful as a gazelle. She dishes out sideways slightly in the near

fore, but that wouldn't be bad even in a riding pony, for a brood mare that should be of no worry, unless she passes it on to her progeny."

The woman tottered past, she was beginning to wheeze.

"We'll keep her running a bit more, its obviously doing her good," said the Captain considerately.

"Now, the seventh thing that I look for is to see if the animal has the qualities particularly suited – or unsuited – for what it is to be used, whether it's for a nervous child in a traffic-filled suburb,

. . . . it's obviously doing her good . . .

or as a hunter for a beefy farmer, as a work-horse for an orchard keeper or as part of a four-in-hand in driving competitions, or to be used for jumping, racing, trekking or whatever. Now, you want it for breeding, I can tell you that she is a good little animal and likely to pass on good qualities to any of her foals, I cannot tell you if she is fertile, that you will have to find out from her stud record. I should buy her."

The owner had stopped out of earshot: her eyes were glazed, she was rocking on her heels and her chest heaved as she gulped breath into her lungs, she looked as if she had just taken part in a Bacchanalian orgy. Before going up to her the Captain said, almost to himself, "'Let your speech be always with grace, seasoned with salt': Paul to the Colossians."

He doffed his hat to the owner and nodded condescendingly towards the mare.

"What a dear little person, you must be fond of her."

The colour drained from the owner's face.

"And some people may not even notice that scar on her hock or the dishing when she runs."

The woman lowered her head in shame.

"I expect that you are asking about £200 for her."

The advertisement had said £450. So crushed was the owner that all she said was:

"Well, we did think we would get £300."

A kindly smile lit up the Captain's features, making them look even more macabre than usual, and he gazed upon the woman with benevolence.

"How charming," he said, and then, still staring at her with his horrible kindly smile, said nothing. She began to shuffle about uneasily.

"Well, what will you offer?"

"Perhaps, so as not to disappoint you, and as it is wearing a nice head collar, £220."

She looked dubious. "I paid £280 for her, and I was told that I should get at least that back, if not more; I should really try and see what I would get at the auction."

The Captain looked urbane, but I'd seen his eyebrow flick. He shook his head sadly:

"Dog-food prices, I'm afraid, that's all they're getting at this sale so far. Tell you what, we will buy it for your £280, presuming her Pedigree Registration Certificates and Vet's papers are satisfactory."

The sale was completed.

"Poor woman," said the Captain, a trifle shame-faced, after the seller had stomped away, bearing our cheque, "'as easy as shooting fish in a barrel', as our American friends say."

Later in the day we bought another mare at the auction. The Captain bid on our behalf using his normal method of signalling, as arranged with the auctioneer: he wore his old steel-rimmed spectacles until the price was no longer acceptable.

We went to celebrate in the stockmen's bar, a tent full to seam-splitting with shouting people: bargaining, boasting, mourning or merry-making. The Captain graciously but gloomily accepted the drink that I had bought him, raised his glass to Dominie, gave her a formal little peck of a bow and recited:

> "He that buys land; buys many stones.
> He that buys flesh; buys many bones.
> He that buys eggs; buys many shells.
> But he that buys good ale; buys nothing else."

CHAPTER 6

Breeding and Birth

Eleazar begat Phinehas, Phinehas begat Abishua,
And Abishua begat Bukki, and Bukki begat Uzzi,
And Uzzi begat Zerahiah, and Zerahiah begat Meraioth,
Meraioth begat Amariah, and Amariah begat Ahitub,
And Ahitub begat Zadok, and Za . . .

I Chronicles 6 iv–viii

In the middle of the yard there was a whirlwind of dust surrounded by a hail of gravel. Shouts, neighs, screams and the trampling of hooves could be heard coming from the centre of the mini-cyclone. The occasional hand or hoof, face or fetlock, bra or bridle could be seen in clearer patches of the dust. Beth scuttled around the mêlée in a crouched, crab-like manner. She was peering into the middle and shouting: "He's in – no he's not, he missed – he's gone too low – he's there – he's poking her tail up, walk her forward – he's out – he's trying again."

A solemn and intent file of children stood on the lane and watched with candid curiosity. They were eventually joined by a gaunt and stern-faced man in jeans and a be-labelled anorak who was shepherding two limping stragglers from the school outing. He took one look at the scene and strode up to us.

"Is this revolting exhibition really necessary?" he snapped primly.

"If you want babies, you have to have sex," I replied.

62

"Why can't you leave them to do it alone, in the privacy of their pastures?"

I began politely to explain, but he strode off, rigid with disdain.

In the beginning, we'd all thought as he did. Unlike some domesticated animals, turkeys, for example, ponies have not been bred into such weird and unnatural shapes that they are physically unable to pair. In fact part of the excellence of the native breeds is based on their origins from herds ruled by that simple law of Nature, "the survival of the fittest". The best stallions produce the most numerous and hardiest offspring. However this free and unmonitored love life is not acceptable to the strict specifications of the official records – the stud books of each breed. These involve rules which insist that matings must be recorded and that no other stallions may have the chance of impregnating a mare. In addition to all this, ponies can be as nervous or as fastidious as human beings. Dominie has had fussy stallions, pernickety mares, ponies which look perfectly normal to the human eye but which are seemingly most unattractive to ponies of the opposite sex, callow colts, frigid fillies and even lesbian mares.

Even when the ponies are mentally at ease, sometimes they are not so physically. One of the main problems concerns the height of the happy – or unhappy – pair. Occasionally Dominie tries to breed down in size, with a large mare being given to a smaller stallion. This results in the poor little fellow having to stand on the tips of his hooves. She has overcome this problem by having a large mound of earth piled up by Wastewood barn: the stallion stands on top of his homemade launching pad in excited anticipation whilst the mare is backed towards him.

A more common physical problem is the habit, which many mares have, of tottering forward under the weight of the stallion during the proceedings thus, as Mr Ryan puts it, "uncorking the bottle". In these cases I hold the mare in a sort of neck lock and push her back, rather like the first row in a rugger scrum. This can be disconcerting, as one comes eyeball-to-eyeball with the stallion and one can see, by his expression, that he is thinking, "Hello, what's that feller doing at the other end?" So frequent are the occasions when I do this that it has become an "in thing" locally: I heard Never-Sweat Siskins, the village sloth, saying to Hot-Hands Honeyball, who was eyeing a maiden bicycling past, "Shall I hold her by the neck for you, Hot-Hands?"

. . . . eyeball-to-eyeball with the stallion . . .

The whole undertaking is extremely exhausting and I was therefore very pleased when Dominie placed a miniature bottle of brandy on the stable wall before the nuptials began. "Good," I thought, "at least she realises what a lot of effort it takes struggling with these stupid mares." When the marriage had been consummated I handed over the bride to Monk, who was standing by, offering advice to all present, including the stallion, and made a bee-line for the brandy bottle. Its destoppered mouth was just being up-ended over mine when Dominie screamed, "Hey! What are you doing with Bugail's brandy?"

"Bugail's?" I shouted. "What's he want it for? He's the one who's been enjoying all this."

"He is very old and has a weak heart, he needs it as a pep-up."

I gave an icy glare at the pampered beast and sped indoors before it could get in and pinch my favourite slippers and armchair.

We had originally approached the subject of breeding with a certain amount of coyness and a great deal of ignorance. To begin with, Bumble Bee was too young – stallions should be at least two years old before they start – and so the stud's involvement in breeding involved the choosing of the correct stallion from another stud, boxing the mare, driving it over to the stallion's home and then collecting it after three or four weeks.

However, the day finally came when our ponies could do their own mating at home.

Mr Ryan was present as a general giver of advice. His first suggestion was that we should choose an experienced mare who had been served several times before because she would be more likely to help the innocent and callow stallion. "Every young man needs an older woman to start with," he said, much to the disapproval of Mrs Pipkin, who was ironing in the kitchen when he said it, and who had some terrible stories to relate about the youths who had approached her recently with that very thought in mind.

Fancy was accordingly led out into the yard by me: I was almost as worried as if I had invented the whole process and kept murmuring words to her in a placatory manner. She looked bored.

"The first thing to do," said Mr Ryan, "is to make sure she is in season." I therefore had to back Fancy to the stable gate. Bumble Bee stood on the other side of it with Dominie holding him by a natty new bridle and lunging rein. He looked over the gate and gave a scream of excited surprise. Fancy replied by putting her ears back and giving the gate a bone-breaking kick.

"Is her vulva working?" asked Mr Ryan.

"Working?" replied Dominie, repelled.

"Sort of twitching and winking."

Beth, who was standing by, blushed.

Bumble Bee gave another sniff and another scream, the mare kicked again and then staled: I was enveloped in clouds of rancid steam. The stallion looked downcast and tried to get back to his stall.

"She's a bit flighty, he being so young," said Mr Ryan. "This is the best way to see if her time is right." He then rolled up the sleeve of his right arm and to the unanimous disgust of all present plunged his arm up to the elbow into the mare's behind. He then withdrew it and offered his hand, black with diesel oil and grease, to the stallion.

"Here, smell this."

Bumble Bee looked at his offering with fastidious scorn and put his ears back.

"Put them together and we'll see what happens," said Mr Ryan.

Beth opened the stable gates and Dominie very gingerly released Bumble Bee, paying him out at the end of the fifteen-foot lunging rein.

"Your rein is too long!" shouted Mr Ryan – too late. Bumble Bee gave a couple more screams of excitement, whirled round, entangled himself in the rein and fell to the ground with a thump.

After the disarray had been unscrambled, Bumble Bee was led once again to the mare, on a tighter rein. He walked past her interesting end and snuffled inquisitively into my face.

"Not me, you bloody fool," I said.

He reared up and, having put his front legs athwart the mare's back, peered vacantly across her like Hay-seed Harry looking over a gate.

"He doesn't know where to stand or where to put it," said Mr Ryan, "here, Beth, look underneath him and see what's happening."

Beth goggled under and then bobbed up, looking rather pink.

"I think he is interested," she said.

Mr Ryan got a long-handled stable broom and pushed the stallion's hindquarters into position; he then also looked underneath.

"He's a bit too short-legged for her, I'll take hold of her head and you will have to direct him into the right place."

Dominie looked at him in squeamish horror.

"Touch *it*?" she exclaimed.

Bradawl, who had arrived a few minutes earlier for his elevenses and who had been watching the drama with pleased interest said that he had an idea. His disappeared into the nearby hedge and re-emerged after a minute bearing a forked stick which he had whittled from a length of blackthorn. Dominie gingerly placed the fork under the stallion's "Mr Pardon", as Beth called it – and pricked it with a thorn that Bradawl had failed to remove.

Bumble Bee gave a squeal of surprised pain and slithered off the mare; she gave him a hefty kick in the chest and we all retired to the stables or the kitchen.

We emerged from the kitchen half an hour later with gritted teeth and determined expressions, Dominie wearing rubber gloves. In the stables, the two ponies had obviously been thinking it over, for after we had led them out they performed as if they were old hands at the game; after that, Dominie was able to release them together in a paddock and they had a long and fruitful honeymoon.

The stallion which gave us the most unexpected problems was Zeno, a venerable grey of a very ancient lineage. His blood line was particularly pleasing to Dominie because it included a great number of the genes of Dyoll Starlight who was born in 1894 and registered number 4 in the stud book. It was he who was largely responsible for changing the colour of the Welsh Mountain Pony from a predominance of "camouflage" colours – duns, bays and browns – to greys. In spite of his age, Zeno had hardly ever bred before he came to us, for he had worked in the most humiliating and frustrating of all jobs: he had been a teaser.

A teaser is a poor unfortunate who is used to do all the wooing. Having galvanised the mare into the correct state of lustful expectancy he is whipped away and some luckier horse is hustled on to the scene to do the actual mating. The teaser saves the complicated bother of getting a thoroughbred stallion ready just to test out if the mare is in season. In addition some of the courtship and preliminaries with a large and skittish pair of thoroughbreds can be dangerous for all those present.

As a result of over twenty years' continual frustration Zeno had developed a hang-dog look. His shoulders were vast and heavily muscled, his massive neck curved in a great crest, his mane and tail were long and flowing, but his eyes stared gloomily at the ground and his walk was a listless amble.

He could not believe his luck when Dominie led him to his first pony mare. She was beautiful and graceful but lacked a certain robustness and substance which Dominie expects to see in a native breed. Zeno's genes should (and did) give an extra sturdiness to her progeny. The stallion ambled up to her, giving me a polite nod as he passed, stared deeply into her eyes, snuffled into her nostrils, gave a couple of stamps and a scream and then stared glumly at Dominie, waiting to be led away. As Dominie made no move he turned back to re-inspect the mare.

"Hello," he seemed to be saying as he sniffed her face, "you're a nice little one, much more my size and shape than those skinny giantesses I'm always being introduced to."

He gave a crafty look at Dominie and me. We deliberately avoided looking back.

"My goodness, if I'm cunning, I might get away with it," he thought.

Carefully he tiptoed to the business end of the mare. He inspected it with the immense gratification and know-how of a connoisseur, like a Tzarina looking at one of Fabergé's latest eggs; then he put his forehooves on her back as lightly as a footman laying a plate of turtle soup before the Lord Mayor of London. He gave us another furtive glance. All of us, including the mare, tried to look unconcerned.

With a yell of "yippee!", after thinking about it for almost two decades, he finally "undertook the act" – as Dr Kinsey says.

By the end of the breeding season he had served twelve mares and had been let out into his winter paddock with a small herd of his own. The boost to his self-confidence and his morale was enormous. No longer did he slink about looking crestfallen. His head was erect, his eyes flashed. When he walked, his feet flicked out at each proud step so that he seemed to float across the pastures.

But his problems were not over. Monique Fewmet met her woolly-minded admirer Mrs Softjoy at the Suffolk Show. "I hear that you have had your palomino mare served by old Zeno," she sibilated.

"Yes," affirmed Mrs Softjoy, smugly.

"Pity he's sterile," snided Monique.

"Sterile?" squawked Mrs Softjoy.

"Oh yes. Has been for years. That's why he was only a teaser. I couldn't understand why he wasn't put down when he was no longer needed. Still, just as well that he's sterile. He's a most peculiar, square, common shape. That crude look has been bred out years ago."

Mrs Softjoy went panicking over to Dominie and repeated the conversation:

". . . and I'm sure she must be right, because she's said it to ever so many other people, and she's ever so knowledgeable, and she . . ."

Dominie's red hair went up like a mane with rage. Her teeth ground audibly across the show-ring. I was reminded how the Romans thought that of all their enemies, the British women were the most frightening and bloodthirsty.

Later, when she had simmered down, she decided to kill the Fewmet rumour by getting a written confirmation of fertility from a vet. Mr Tomkins was called. He is one of the world's experts on assessing the potency and breeding qualities of stallions, and he travels all over the world in the course of his occupation.

He came accompanied by a leather tube, three foot long, with a rubber bag at one end, a hole at the other and a complication of buckles and straps in between. It was the artificial mare used to collect the stallion's semen.

"It can be very difficult, telling people what this is for," he complained. "Last time I went through the customs in Naples Airport, no one seemed to understand English so I had to explain its purpose with gestures and drawings. I don't know what they eventually thought, but they all queued up to shake me by the hand."

He disappeared modestly into Zeno's stall; two weeks later the stallion received a letter telling him that he was not sterile and, furthermore, he had an "excellent libido".

Although I lived on a farm all my childhood, I did not see much of the process of birth: the occasional cow could be discerned calving in a distant field; a cat, absent for some days, would appear from the recesses of a barn with a kindle of kittens; Mickey and Minnie, my mundanely-named mice, routinely produced a squirmful of pink jelly-babies in their nest of cottonwool and newspaper. Even when our first child, Henrietta, was born, I knew little of the proceedings because Dominie, suspecting that the whole thing would be unattractive and messy, sent me away to have breakfast with a friend who, in consideration of my slight agitation, gave me an excellent meal. I returned to the hospital sated with porridge, eggs, bacon, fried bread, sausages, kidneys, toast and marmalade, all washed down with Black Velvet. It was therefore slightly groggily that I viewed a smiling wife holding a glossily pristine baby, the whole tableau ensconced neatly between starched white sheets and prettily surrounded with flowers.

Birth, I decided, was a perfectly natural and pleasant undertaking, the details of which were best left to women, who seemed interested in them. The arrival of George, our second child, put an end to these chauvinist opinions.

We were living in Yorkshire then, during my time as a Rayon salesman. Our house, although one of the oldest in Northern Britain, built about a thousand years ago, had surprisingly few records of children being born there. The celibate shepherd monks of Fountains Abbey had used it as a rest house for four hundred years, it was used as a church for a couple of centuries, had had periods of abandonment and had acted as a home for war-wounded. The only child that we knew of who had been born there came into the busy world of Tudor England, and she was busier than most, being obliged to toddle up the aisle at the age of three to get married, becoming a widow when nine, then getting the Pope's dispensation to marry her brother-in-law, which she did a few months later, thus becoming the Duchess of Cumberland.

When we lived there, most of our neighbouring dalesfolk had been brought into the world by Doctor Cameron and his team, Sister Bonnet and Sister Sparks. The doctor was a man of gentle charm and immaculate neatness, never did I see his tie-pin askew nor his smooth, straight hair unbrushed. All that he did was undertaken with the calm confidence of fifty years' experience.

"Have your baby at home, it's more natural and much nicer for both mother and baby," he urged soothingly. Dominie agreed.

On the great day a large cast had assembled: Dominie and I, of course, Doctor Cameron and Sister Bonnet; Sister Walker, a briskly efficient maternity nurse who was to look after the mother and child for the first month; Mrs Morden who "came to help"; Harry and Sue Grousebutt, who had been married in London the day before and who had decided to drop in unexpectedly and stay the night on the way to their honeymoon yacht anchored off Oban, and finally Xerxes Pothanger, a passing rambler, who spent most of the time in a tent on the lawn.

The labour lasted fifteen hours and, from the moment when it started so dramatically, every minute seemed a nightmare of activity.

Just before it all began the scene was of idyllic peace: home-coming crows crooned quietly to their young in the nests that swayed at the tops of the trees surrounding the house, the setting sun created a gold patch of gothic-shaped light on the wall opposite the kitchen window, Mrs Morden's knitting needles clicked comfortably as she sat on the rocking chair beside the stove, and the air was filled with a pleasant, warm smell blended from the scents of scones baking in the oven and of ironed linens as Sister Walker prepared nappies and sheets for the anticipated event.

Dominie bent down to look at the scones, clapped her hands to her sides and cried, "Ouch! I think it's started."

The door bell rang and tweedy voices cried, "Hello there, hello there! Surprise! Surprise! Is anybody at home?"

A picture fell off the wall and Mrs Morden screeched, "My God! That means a death in the house!"

Sister Walker, normally so efficient, put her iron down on a bed-sheet in her haste both to help Dominie and remonstrate with Mrs Morden, and the sheet began to smoulder.

There was a hesitant tapping on the window and a peaky, wistful face bobbed up and down behind the glass shouting, in an anxious American accent, "Pardon me for the intrusion, but may I indulge in the convenience of your water faucet and sanctity from the elements within your garden wall?"

I felt dizzy and faint.

Sister Walker suggested that I help Dominie upstairs to bed, it was only when we were halfway up that we realised that it was she who was helping me up. I had even developed a doubled-over posture and an expression of anguish. Having put her to bed I rushed over to the telephone and bellowed down it: "It's started! Come over! It's here, quick! For God's sake, hurry . . .!"

"How many seconds between each contraction?" asked the voice at the other end.

"About thirty or forty."

"Ring me back in three hours," replied the doctor, and put the receiver down.

The rambler was shown a nook wherein to pitch his tent, the Grousebutts disappeared into the spare bedroom, guffawing sheepishly, Sister Walker kept boiling things, Mrs Morden went up the cobbled High Street to cook dinner for her family and I was set to work by Dominie to cook our own dinner – a task I undertook with fretful incompetence.

Three hours later the doctor wandered in, inspected Dominie, and drifted downstairs. "Keep me informed," he said to Sister Walker. "It won't be for a few hours yet; she's got good child-bearing hips but looks the sort who might need forceps."

"What will you do if the mother or baby get into distress?"

"Same as always, a pad of ether for the mother, a slap on the bottom if it's a baby girl, a cold bath if it's a boy."

Sister Walker looked aghast at the primitiveness of it.

By seven o'clock next morning we knew the baby had stuck.

"No matter," said the doctor cheerily to Sister Bonnet who, true to her name, had bustled about efficiently for two hours without once removing the shapeless black blob that she wore on her head, "we'll induce a bit of muscular effort." A roller towel was tied to one of the footposts of the four-poster bed in which Dominie lay and at the cheerful shout from doctor and sister for "One – Two – Three – Heave!" she pulled with all her might at the towel; the poor bed, 400 years old, creaked and groaned with anguish under the strain, like a tumbril being driven down a flight of stairs.

I sat in the kitchen for the next two hours hearing, every twenty seconds, the cries of "One – Two – Three – Heave", then the rickety noises of the bed. People came and went with bowls of boiling water, wet towels and hot-water bottles. I began to feel appallingly guilty.

Suddenly, instead of the normal cacophony, I heard other noises, those of slappings and the doctor's voice saying, "Wake up! Wake up!" Then a thin wailing filled the air.

I bounded up the stairs, Dominie lay back in bed, her eyes shut. The doctor was flipping her cheeks fore and aft with an elegant hand. Sister Walker was staring alternately with horrified disapproval at a chloroformed pad which the doctor must have tossed at the foot of the bed, and with rapt admiration at the doctor. Sister Bonnet, looking pleased, was holding one of the most repulsive objects I have ever seen, about the size and shape of a large marrow, purplish, sticky and screeching like a banshee. Dominie opened her eyes, looked at the results of her labours with a quick glance, looked at me, said, "I don't think I want any more babies," and went to sleep.

She had changed her mind by the time she woke up.

So it was with a certain feeling of irony that I observed Dominie's behaviour during the birth of her first foal. The mother was Santilla, a particularly beautiful four-year-old cream, which Dominie had bought in foal, after the mare had been mated with a chestnut stallion called Revel Harmonic. The birthplace was in the stables just next to the house. Dominie had seen that the birth was imminent as the mare's udders started to "wax up" (gobbets of white, waxy substance appeared at the end of the teats) and had therefore taken her off the pasture and ensconced her in a nice clean stall with fresh straw on the floor and plenty of clean water.

The first sign that she saw of the actual birth taking place was of the mare staring round worriedly at her behind. Dominie's eyes followed those of the pony's and she saw, with a jump in her heart, that a small hoof had appeared. Mr Whippletree was summoned with frantic telephone calls; Tony Crisp and I were sent for; Dominie paced up and down, wringing her hands. The foal was born with no difficulty within half an hour. All that Mr Whippletree had to do was to pull the cowl off the newborn's face: "Might as well do this as I'm here, if it doesn't get away from the foal's nostrils it may suffocate it and it can sometimes set as stiff as a sheet of plastic." He checked the foal for its sex – it was a filly – and told Dominie to remove the afterbirth when it was shed, and, if this did not appear before four o'clock, to telephone him.

Nearly all our foalings have been as simple but we have had five problem cases: two foals had to be put down, one with a malformed leg and another which could not stand and seemed mentally distressed, perhaps it had been kicked in the head during birth. We had a still-birth, a bad "presentation", and one case of misadoption, which caused a lot of trouble and expense.

This problem arose because of "herding". It is always interesting to see the behaviour of these herds, for when animals are put into a group their individual personality sometimes changes to the benefit of the group itself which develops a character of its own. This can even be seen with humans: some classes at school are known to be difficult in comparison to others; one workshop in a factory can have a high morale, another can be full of glum and discontented employees; one football club be known for the loutishness of its supporters, another for their good temper.

The most simple of Dominie's herds are the "men-only" groups, which consist of the yearling and two-year-old colts and stallions. I had presumed that stallions fight when put together, but Dominie learned that this is unlikely, with Welsh Mountain Ponies, at least, if there are no mares present to start up an aggressive rivalry. If there are only two or three stallions they often become friends; if there are more, a "pecking order" is usually assumed through the use of a few bites and threatening gestures. Once each stallion has decided upon his status in the group, he then settles down to a life of amiable unity with his companions. There are exceptions: those few stallions who cannot abide colts. Bumble Bee, although the most gentle of stallions, was only put with colts twice – each time he tried to savage them.

It is often surprising to see who has forced himself to the top of the social heap, for it is not necessarily the strongest or the oldest and most experienced. For example, Dominie once put five stallions together: old Flute, aged 23, Madryn, aged 18, Springbok, the big palomino aged 20, Poppy, the youngest at 7, and the largest, Herbert, a nondescript cob of around 10 which Mr Ryan had swapped for a waggon-load of parsnips and two hundred-weight of copper piping. One of the oldest and most burly of the stallions, Springbok, was at the bottom of the pecking order and had to wait for the others to finish the daily winter feed bonus of pony nuts and bruised oats before he could move in and take his share. This was in spite of the fact that he had once commanded a large and semi-wild herd of his own mares and foals in the Welsh mountains. Perhaps age had taught him that the trivialities of life are not worth fighting over but, had Dominie introduced a mare to the group, he would have beaten his companions into submission.

Dominie tries to have three or family herds on the estate. Each of these consists of pregnant brood mares, their unweaned foals, a single stallion and the mares which are to be bred with that stallion. Even the most docile of stallions, like Bumble Bee, becomes very much the defender of the herd. An angry stallion is an awesome sight: he puts his head down a foot above the ground and parallel to it, stretches his neck out into a serpentine posture and hunches his shoulders up into a rearing crest, he then glides towards his enemy with small but mincingly rapid paces. A horse bite can take a chunk of flesh off any person, a kick from a rear leg can break an oaken gate, a kick from a front leg can slice the top off a human skull as effectively as a spoon through an eggshell. The stallion usually controls his herd with threatening gestures and nips, never by kicking. Kicks are the privilege of his mares, when he oversteps his position and becomes flirtatious when they are not in season, but he never retaliates to these rebuffs. The foals hold him in dread, particularly the fillies, but the braver colts may play with him, first approaching him with a sign of submission, an exaggerated mouthing which resembles a political broadcast on the television with the noise turned off. The games are somewhat simple, usually a lap or two run round the stallion and then a breathtaking gallop back to the other foals with a "Haven't I been brave" attitude.

The final type of herd is made up of the remnants: the riding ponies, fillies too young to breed and stock being set aside for breaking as riding or driving ponies.

I was taught, as an anthropologist, that most groups of humans include a set cast of stock characters: the leader, the *éminence grise*, the buffoon or joker, the scapegoat-cum-outcast, and the protector. A herd of ponies is obviously less complex; nevertheless there is always a leader and often a scapegoat and a protector. Dominie has not yet fathomed out what causes a pony to become an outcast. It does not seem to have anything to do with personality or health, but the evidence is always the same: a pony, always female, standing dejectedly outside the general mass of the herd and always being the last to get food or find shelter in bad weather. The protectors, "nannies", Dominie calls them, can be useful. She looks to see which pony seems inclined to defend the others from attack or is allowed by the mares to act as babysitter for their foals, and then takes this kindly soul to stay for a few days with a pony who is about to join the herd, perhaps a newcomer or one who has been in quarantine. Then, when the animal has been released into the pasture, it is protected by its benevolent friend from much of the standard chasing, chivvying and abuse which are the normal ordeal of a new arrival to a herd – or school – or platoon – or workshop – or boardroom.

★ ★ ★

Dominie puts most of her pregnant mares in nursery fields, together with the stallion she has chosen for those particular mares. There the young are born and grow up together and in doing so learn communal life, how to behave towards their elders and to their contemporaries. They become strong and nimble by playing together and they can be defended by the adults in the herd from the most brutal of all vermin, the rogue dog and the human lout. This communal living can sometimes be inconvenient if there are over-possessive "nannies" in the herd, mares who have not yet foaled and who try to satisfy their frustrated mother love by forcibly adopting the progeny of other mares. The best way of overcoming this is by removing them until they have a foal of their own. A worse problem once occurred when two mares decided to foal at the same time and in the same corner of the field. When they finally took note of their surroundings after their labours they both decided that the little colt was theirs and the little filly the other's. They jostled each other about, kept possessively thrusting the unfortunate colt away from their rival, hurried up and down the field with it sandwiched between them and utterly ignored the sad little filly. Dominie overcame the first problem by choosing one of the mares at random, wiping the filly with the mare's after-birth and shutting them up together in a stall for a day. The other problem concerned the stud book: who could be registered as the dam? Registering the sire was no problem, for he was father to both foals. Mr Whippletree took samples from the mares and foals and sent them to the Newmarket Equine Research Station. They were particularly kind and said that they would not charge Dominie if they could not help her. They sent her a bill, for they did manage to confirm who had foaled which through a series of blood tests.

Our most irksome problem birth was with a mare who had the same trouble as Dominie had with George, the foal stuck. Unfortunately, it happened at a weekend when we had house guests and had asked other friends for dinner to meet them. Dominie had suspected that all was not well with the mare and had asked Mr Whippletree to have a look at her. Halfway through dinner he appeared and came up to me as I was sitting blandly at the head of the table, chatting up the female guests and enjoying Dominie's cooking. He hissed at me: "I need you at once, it is a lumbo-sacral presentation." I hadn't a clue what he was talking about. Later I learned that the foal was upside down and back to front, but the sight of his slime-covered hands and dung-covered knees convinced my previously giggly and pleasant dining partners that he and I should leave at once.

I stood in the stable, my patent leather shoes flinching disdainfully from various steaming heaps. "Hold her hard by the head, every time she strains I will have to pull at her foal and perhaps position it within her."

The mare was standing, looking downcast and sweaty. I wrapped my dinner-jacketed arms about her neck, dug my heels into the floor and heaved her to my chest. Wearing the same clothes, I used to do the same thing at deb dances, but somehow the thrill had gone out of it. At the other end of the mare Mr Whippletree intermittently rummaged, heaved and searched. He reminded me of a foreign diplomat I had once sat next to on a train journey: he had spent much of the time going frenziedly through his document case of state papers, looking for his misplaced copy of *Playboy*.

After about ten minutes Mr Whippletree gave a low cry of gratification and staggered into view from behind the mare's rump, bearing a large and greasy bundle: "Mother and child will be all right," he panted. Mother disagreed, she gave a deep sigh, buckled at the knees and fell sleepily on top of me.

Just then Dominie and the rest of the dinner party arrived and peered fastidiously over the stable door. In one corner Mr

. . . . panting peacefully . . .

Whippletree sat, smothered in sweat and goo and holding a damp foal on his lap. In the other corner the mare lay, panting peacefully. From one side of her a pair of evening shoes protruded, neatly side by side, on the other lay my resentful head and shoulders, my bow tie still in shape on my shirt but my features rapidly empurpling.

Dominie smiled gratefully at Mr Whippletree: "Thank you so much, there's a sinkful of hot water waiting for you, and then do come and join us and finish the port." She glanced at me, kindly but firmly: "You really must come on in instead of lying there, you've got guests to entertain."

CHAPTER 7

Riding and Control

At her feet he bowed, he fell, he lay down:
at her feet he bowed, he fell:
where he bowed, there he fell . . .

Judges 5 xxvii

Perhaps because I am not one hundred per cent English I have three strong differences with my fellow countrymen: I dislike tea – unless it is blended with rum and drunk out of a mess tin – I loathe watching other people playing games and I do not instantly dote upon dogs when they come fawning and grinning to abase themselves at my feet. I like most working dogs, such as sheepdogs and blind-guides, and I like pugs and pekineses: I am convinced that there is no "yellow peril" from China, no race of people who can invent anything as charmingly useless as pugs or pekineses can be anything but peaceful and eccentric at heart. (Perhaps the heartbroken people of Tibet would not agree, come to think of it.) Now that I am over fifteen stone and have won the bale-throwing competition in a local village show I can admit my penchant for certain lap-dogs. At school I dared not confess that my mother had a honey-coloured peke called Snuff-Snuff; instead I pretended we had large Teutonic dogs like Alsatians and those repulsive, dribbly curs whose tails are cut off so that you can see more of their behinds. I do not entirely approve of many dogs; I think that the kangaroos and dolphins which they eat in vast quantities are better seen hopping or swimming about rather than as skidded-on eyesores on pavements.

One pet I have always liked is the parrot. My father had one. She developed an extraordinary sequence of noises: a tinkle, a trickle, some whooshing, a seething and finally a few gulpings. We finally realised that she was imitating Papa dealing with a gin and tonic. I greatly envied a school friend, many years ago, who not only had a mad aunt, but had one with a bald parrot. It was as bald as a stone and was quite the most disgusting creature I had ever seen, its blotched, pinky-blue nudity accentuated by a small tuft of red and grey feathers on top of its head, like an Ascot hat, and its parson's nose, although devoid of feathers, sparsely be-whiskered with a few silky hairs. People seemed unable to resist sticking their fingers through the bars of its cage and prodding the bird, which would then half-close its eyes in bliss, gently take the end joint of the prying finger in its beak and suddenly crack it like a walnut. After the ensuing screams had been soothed into mere sobs the mad aunt would don an elegant doeskin glove, ornamented from wrist to elbow with a row of mother-of-pearl buttons, pick up a small hunting crop, kept handy for the purpose, and chastise the parrot on its naked behind.

As a child, I had few animals: a guinea-pig which was eaten by Rags, my father's mongrel, two exceedingly phlegmatic goldfish, Finny and Fanny, Mickie and Minnie the mice and finally Tatters, my charming but grossly ugly Staffordshire bull terrier. The presence of a pony blighted much of my childhood. It was a New Forest, a bay mare, rather fat and about 13.2 hands which, when I was only 10 hands, seemed terribly high; I greatly envied my brother, Sam, on Tom Thumb, his Shetland, who seemed to be a much safer distance from the ground. Big Sam, the gardener and groom, used to detest Polly even more than I did for she was a kicker and so he had to tie a red ribbon on to her tail to warn everyone not to go behind her: he tied this ribbon on very gingerly, and at arm's length. Unlike Big Sam and me, the mare loved to go hunting. When out she would go frantic with excitement and determination to keep up with the rest of the field. I remember many occasions as I bobbed upon her back whilst we sped over the ploughland, Big Sam panting beside me as he dragged on the leading rein, and then his despairing curses as we approached a hedge and finally soared in triplicate over it. By the time I had learned to ride properly Big Sam could have won the Olympic hurdles.

Like most small boys, I was an uneasy, fretful little creature, full of secret fears and thoughts of abasement, and the fount of many of these lachrymose sentiments was girl riders. They were so keen, and they were so good. They fettled and foraged and curried and combed and knickered and knackered and did all the right sort of things for their pony's health and welfare after each ride. I merely hopped off my horrible Polly and hurried away, leaving all the ensuing tedium to Big Sam. They loved riding bareback with their arms crossed and endlessly practised jumping over striped poles and oil drums; they went to see *National Velvet* sixteen times and blubbed at all the right places; they avidly read amazingly tedious books like *My Friend Flicka*, *The Famous Five go Trekking* and *A Pony for Jane*. They talked with authority and pleasure about incomprehensible things such as hackamores, half-holts, hobdays and *hautes écoles*; they asked Father Christmas for tins of hoof oil and some pony nuts "'cos we tried so hard, we really did, at the Tendring Hundred Show" and signed the letter with names like "Pru and Trotters".

I kept falling off.

I knew, I really did, that boys were big, strong and manly whilst girls were simpering weeds, prone to screaming at insects and hopeless at rugger. Great was my chagrin, therefore, at the excellence and enthusiasm of their riding. The worst of the lot was Griselda Aigrish, a handsome girl when dressed in her pony club livery and seated astride her big black Fell pony (thought a bit less attractive when glowering from the frilly neck of a party frock). Every time I went out hunting she would dash past me, at the same time tipping my hat over my eyes and screaming, "Hurry up, old slowcoach!" Mr Ryan's theory is that the human male has a less well developed sense of balance than the female and is more top-heavy, having longer legs and a smaller behind. It is only at about the age of fifteen, when they became muscular, that boys can at last ride as well as girls, but even then they have to use more physical effort.

One day, when I was twelve, my father summoned me to his study and said sadly, avoiding my eyes, "I'm sorry to tell you that your pony has just died." I could not contain a sudden yelp of exhilaration, which he mistook for regret, and it was with difficulty that I dissuaded him from buying me a replacement. I had little to do with riding after that: the odd weekend when, drat it, my host would say, "We've got a spare horse so you can come out with us," and a period of expensive madness when I tried to learn polo.

The incompetence of my horsemanship was confirmed when I started to play this game. I was courting Dominie at the time: her father had his own polo team and her eldest brother, who was at Cambridge with me, was a half-blue and played for the university. Many of my competitors for Dominie's affections had annoying whinneying laughs, horsey faces and kept casually whirling their right arms round in anti-clockwise movements and then grunting, "Wham!" as they hit imaginary polo balls with imaginary sticks. All these clues suggested that Dominie must dote on anything to do with polo and therefore if I played the game, I cunningly reasoned, she would dote upon me as well.

I was wrong, she had become rather annoyed by the hard seats of Smiths Lawn and, as she wore her specs only in secret, as she thought them unbecoming, she never saw a thing anyhow. Ignorant of this, I accordingly strolled up to the youth whom I had decided would become my brother-in-law and asked him how I could learn to play polo.

"To play properly," he said unsympathetically, "you should buy yourself a couple of experienced ponies and then, instead of spending your time ogling my sister, learn to ride."

"I can ride," I replied with a certain pique, "but can't afford any ponies," I added.

"Pity, we'll have to let you use one of the club ponies, but we don't like them being ruined by learners. We're having a few practice chukkas the day after tomorrow. Come to the ground in your riding kit, but before that I'll take you to the practice horse and show you the basic strokes so that you can then learn to hit the ball."

The practice horse was rather like a wide wooden trestle; it was saddled and had a neck and head so that one could practise one of the most difficult strokes – a ball coming from the right which must be hit to the left under the pony's neck. The pit it was in was surrounded by wire netting and the sloping floor was boarded so that any ball which was hit automatically rolled down the incline back towards the "rider".

"This is fun," I thought, as I lolled on the saddle, sipping the gin and tonic which a steward had just bought from the adjacent Pitt Club. I patted the wooden neck in front of me, put down my glass and with a languid turn of the wrist sent the ball trundling up the slope in front.

"This is ghastly," I thought, as I zig-zagged over the twelve acres of the Cambridge Polo Ground, next day. "Why can't this bloody nag run in a straight line?"

No one had told me that a polo pony is guided by the feel of reins on the side of its neck opposite to the direction the rider wants to turn. Although I was thus puzzled by my steed's eccentric perambulation to begin with, my puzzlement turned to ire the first time that I tried to hit the ball. It looked an easy shot: the ball was coming straight at me, almost, just a little bit too far out to my right. I leant further out to reach it, pushed my left hand away from me to act as a counter-balance, and in doing so laid my reins on the right side of my pony's neck; thus, as I smote, the pony leapt sideways, away from the ball – which I hit, with the top of my head.

I persevered in my attempts to play polo, spurred on partly by my determination to impress Dominie, partly because I thought I looked rather dashing in my pith helmet and partly inspired by the knowledge that there was a player even worse than I, Harith Kahn. Harith originates from a mountainous part of the Indian sub-continent, near the North-West Frontier. Their local horse is an odd mixture of breeds and includes a bit of Persian, a soupçon of Steppe, a dash of charger and some Hunnic pony. The result is almost like a Barbary ape, able to clamber up rocks, scramble over screes and spring from pinnacle to pinnacle. Harith's main fault as a horseman was his impetuosity. He did not mount in the careful way that I was taught, like someone settling upon a clutch of eggs, he leapt upon his steed and spurred it into action as if he were starting up a motor-bicycle in a TT race; he then urged his pony about the field with excited shouts and wrenchings at the reins, causing the fastidious animal to cavort and sidle like a whirligig beetle on a pond. And he had no sense of balance. Most of his childhood had been spent on horseback, this being the only way of getting about and, in much the same way that a British child is obliged to play football and cricket, so he too was expected to be athletic, but his clan only played one game. He called it *buz-kashi*, but Sergeant Sherrick, an old-soldier friend who knows the area, calls it Snatch-the-Goat and says it is a sort of mounted rugger with no rules, with any number of players and with a stuffed goat instead of a ball. Rumour said that it was during one of these games that Harith lost his left eye, another rumour said that this was the result of an unsuccessful assassination attempt against his father by one of his uncles. Whatever the cause, the result was a horrific scar from a blind eye to a non-existent ear and the complete absence of any sense of balance. He fell off his pony at the slightest opportunity, he even fell off the practice horse, but his cheerful zest seemed in no way abated and his ferocious appearance scared the wits out of our opponents.

The downstairs lavatory is the showplace in many houses: a notice-board upon which are pinned pictures and diplomas which the householders pretend are of such insignificance that they are only fit for use as wallpaper in the most humble room in the house. But it is a room which most guests visit and in which they have time to stand and stare. Sometimes one visits the eccentric who merely hangs up instructions on how to work the antiquated cistern, or has a framed picture of a line of dogs wearing suits and queuing up to use a pissoir. Normally one sees family trees, coats of arms, scrolls from the Pope or the president of the National Farmers Union extolling the fertility of the householder or of his pastures; photographs of a daughter going over the jumps at the local point-to-point, or of a son sitting with arms folded and a belligerent expression with the rest of his school second XV rugger team, or of the householder himself on his yacht proudly holding up the corpse of a huge fish or talking earnestly into the ear of a noticeably bored Prince Philip about a machine, or of his wife wearing a ludicrously out-of-date frock and grotesque hat and presenting a prize to a suitably deferential school child.

Our downstairs loo is full of photographs of our children, highly disconcerting to those of a modest nature, like Mr Ryan's friend Dai Plimsoles who does not wish to use the plumbing under the frank gaze of fifty pairs of coldly critical eyes. We also have an arrangement of implements which include my polo stick, ice axe, squash racquet and fishing trident which show, in a modest but noticeable manner, that I would be able to use these sporty implements, if I wanted to. In fact, the polo stick has hardly a dent upon it: I remained a rotten player and although I enjoyed the game it was to the relief of my ego, my bank manager and my polo pony that I finally hung up my stick. Having done so, I thought that I had finished with riding, probably as a participant, certainly as a spectator. I was wrong, our children forced me back into the horse-competing world. It was the girls, for the boys, having learned to ride, as I told them they must, gave up riding, as I told them they might. The girls, having learned, became besotted, and I was therefore obliged to help, firstly with the pony shows, then with the competitive events and finally with the hunting; the only consolation being that each stage needed less attention.

Pony shows involve the ultimate of neatness combined with immaculate behaviour from both rider and steed. On the eve of each show the pony is washed and combed and polished and, if it is being entered for the lead-rein classes, its mane is plaited into rat-tails, which are then rolled up into little balls and sewn into place. The result is a row of little bobbles extending from ears to withers not, in my opinion, very attractive – I like a horse's tail and mane to be free and flowing. Each child is also cleaned and fettled in her turn: bathed and flannelled, her nails inspected, her hair plaited, her tweed jacket brushed clean of hay-seeds and cake crumbs, tie ironed, boots polished and hat brushed clean from the mud of the last fall. Next day some stubborn little brute of an animal, primped and permed like a starlet's poodle, is hauled into the trailer and then the horse and rider, accompanied by an excited mother and sister, two grizzling brothers and an exasperated father, who would rather be in his garden, truck off to some wind-blasted quagmire where the show is taking place. Nervous tantrums then ensue because a speck of dirt is discerned on a hoof, a hair-net becomes laddered or a glove is missing. Sometimes there is a triumphant return home, with a rosette to be nailed to the inside of the pony's stable door, sometimes the opposite, the maddening memory of a pony staring balefully at a pole suspended a foot above the ground and finally the dreaded words over the loudspeaker: "Thank you, number 14, you can come in now . . . Miss Courtauld is disqualified for her third refusal." The puffy eyes, the hang-dog but defiant pony, the words of consolation and excuse, the enraging condolences from the mother of the winner, usually Monique Fewmet, and finally the maddeningly eager prattle ending

"... and so, Mummy, Noreen says there is another show, next week at Twinstead, can we go, please?"

Events are better, because they are at least remotely interesting to the onlooker. Our girls have been particularly keen on the Tetrathlon, a day-long event which involves swimming, running (usually a mile), shooting (with an air-gun) and riding over an obstacle course. It is rather shaming to see how some fathers become keen about this. Instead of standing about in the approved manner with an expression of aloof indifference mixed with an air of martyrdom, some fathers actually cheer on their children or, even worse, run undignifiedly alongside with stopwatch in hand, bellowing statistics and exhorting greater efforts. Even I can scarcely refrain from the encouraging nod, though I know what to expect every time: our girls are almost always amongst the last of the runners, the first of the swimmers, towards the bottom with the shooting (they close both eyes when they squeeze the trigger) and reasonably up front with the riding.

Then came hunting. Even I, who am not a besotted horseman, have once or twice been overcome in my life by that exhilaration one can have on the hunting field brought on, perhaps, by the primitive excitement of the chase, the comradeship of peril, the

. . . . most hunting people . . .

hollering of the hounds, the thunder of hooves and the speed and the soaring. I sometimes can see an "anti's" point of view, but generally it merely seems the spiteful malice of someone who dislikes those different from himself. I remember a London newspaper having a week's frenetic correspondence on the subject a few years ago. During those five days I hardly read one letter of sympathy for the fox, merely a tirade of spite against the "fox-hunting squires", the "toffee-nosed public school boys", the "chinless wonders", "red-faced Tory farmers" and the "privileged few". I have met some of these, but they are rare, and most hunting people are merely ordinary and harmless people who live in the country and like a bit of exercise and a purpose when they are riding their horses or ponies. Few of them say the fox enjoys it, but, if it were not for hunting, the chicken-loving villager and cat-loving suburbanite would have poisoned all our foxes years ago. We had an invasion of "anti's" at a Boxing Day meet some years ago: they were a brawling, bullying lot. Bigotry and hate spilled from their mouths and sharpened their voices to screeches. Captain Firecrest was with us at the time, to assess a pony he had been asked to buy, and he said to himself as he surveyed the milling, shoving mob: ". . . while the worst are full of passionate intensity".

. . . . are merely ordinary and harmless . . .

Whatever hunting may be like, I am not enamoured of buzzing round the lanes in a car looking worriedly for my mounted offspring to see if they are safe and are not breaking any hunting rules and codes. There are many of these points of etiquette to learn, the most important being to ensure that your mount does not kick a hound, the next, probably, to keep clear of the master and hunt servants. Hunting is also dangerous. Therefore, if possible, children should start out with an experienced rider who is prepared to hang back and look after them. When Henrietta first went out with the hounds neither Dominie nor I had the time or inclination to accompany her so I asked ex-Troop Sergeant Sherrick to look after.

He is a retired non-commissioned officer from one of the Lancer regiments: he had been seconded from the Lancers to become an adviser to the Royal Jordanian Army and liking the country, being a widower and having a daughter married to an expatriate civil engineer who lives in Amman, he decided to retire there. After a time, boredom struck, so he accepted a job of manager of a stud farm owned by a local racing fanatic. He comes to England twice a year: in the winter to spend Christmas with his other daughter, to hunt and to go to the sales at Tattersalls; around June to go to the flat races at Epsom (the Derby and the Oaks) and to Ascot.

He is a small, gingery man, usually dressed in jodhpurs and a polo-necked jersey. His moustache fascinates the children: he buys tins of special wax which he uses to stiffen the ends of his whiskers upwards into two long, sharp points, like the feelers of a prawn. Like many horsemen he is extremely superstitious: he never stands his boots on the floor, for that is symbolic of being dismounted and although he usually relies on his judgement when choosing the winner of a race, if he has any doubts he selects from his list of options with a pin from a wedding dress; whenever any of his employer's horses wins he kisses it, which apparently ensures that it will win again.

The second occasion Henrietta went hunting under the care of the Sergeant resulted in a dramatic confrontation. It was a Saturday, the day we normally shoot at home, so after seeing Henrietta and her pony being driven off to the meet, which was being held about five miles away, I donned my Norfolk jacket, summoned my dog, Potter, and went off to my parents' house to join the rest of the shooting party.

About noon I was in the middle of the line staring into the centre of a wood and hearing from its depths the rattle of sticks against trees as the beaters advanced towards us and Monk's voice occasionally barking out as he brought a flank into line or reproved a laggard or a pusher. Suddenly we heard different barking: more excited and of a baying nature, then cries from the beaters of "Charlie! Charlie!" as the fox ran between them. The fox, a large and grizzled dog, burst out of the wood in front of me, then ran past me and disappeared into the spinney behind. We merely raised our hats, rather than our guns, in acknowledgement and then continued to watch to the front. The baying grew closer, swearing filled the air, Monk's naval vocabulary noticeably to the fore; there was a frantic braying from a hunting horn, the belling of the hounds reached a fortissimo, cursings and shouts from beaters, huntsmen and whippers-in and a huge cloud of pheasants which exploded into the air, a fusillade of shots, the hounds panting past us in a skewbald spate, tails all a-wag, noses well down on the scent, the master and hunt servants scarlet of face and livery and then the followers: old Miss Westly-Waterless and Mrs Flowermead, magnificent in the top-hats and flowing habit of the side-saddle, Parson Holt in black from bowler to boots except for his dog collar, George Junkett, milkman in the morning and AA man in the afternoon, still in the AA uniform and on the horse which pulled his milk float, some people in ratcatchers, others in pink; then a mob of ponies, above them a score of pony club ties and two score of excited bright eyes and looming above them the mounted figures of their guardians: Griselda, now Lady Martinsnest, uttering crisp and imperious instructions, Pamela Rantipole, shiny and hot and holding one of her nieces on a leading rein and Sergeant Sherrick with Henrietta and some other children whom he was tending, milling about his girths. Finally, panting and dishevelled and hysterical with rage and frustration, Millicent and two friends holding banners.

I went to meet the homecomers that evening, as they disembussed from the trailer parked by the stables.

"Did you kill any foxes?" I asked Henrietta.

"Of *course* not!" she said.

CHAPTER 8

A Fishing Interlude

The depth closed me round about,
the weeds were wrapped about my head.
                                    Jonah 2 v

Because it was Lent we could only eat fish: it was salmon which
the monks poached from Loch Ness, or so Brother Patrick the
bee-keeper told us, but he had such an eccentric sense of humour
that we never knew if he was joking or being earnest. Whatever
he said, he always gazed past us into the distance, through steel-
rimmed spectacles, with a little quizzical twinkle which kept us
wondering. We were schoolboy members of a mountain rescue
team and were staying in the monastery, looking for one of the
lay brothers who had been missing for several days. He had last
been seen wandering in the Monadhliath Mountains and so we
spent three weeks searching among those lonely peaks with strange
names sounding like the magic spells chanted by the witches of
Macbeth: Càrn Coire na h-Easgainn, Gael-Chàrn Mór, Beinn
a'Chaoruinn, Meall na h-Aisre and Choc Fraing.

   Full of odd little jests though he was, Brother Patrick was always
solemn when he spoke of Nessie, the Loch Ness Monster. He
swore that he had seen her. "Three humps she has, my boys; they
rise out of the waters as black and as silent as clouds on the horizon
and then speed as rapidly across the loch as did poor John Cobb
in his world-beating motor boat." The other monks would nod in
agreement and we would stare back at them in pleasurable dread.

90

All morning we had been in macabre quest beneath the summer sun, wading through the heather which scratched raw knees bared below our shorts and slipping over the granite scree to where the buzzards circled, like vultures, above corpses. But the corpses we found were only of sheep or of deer. We rested in the snug pockets of moss and heather, eating our monk-packed lunch of chocolate, oranges, buttered baps and home-smoked salmon sandwiches, whilst larks as young as we trilled overhead and the new-sprung waters of the River Findorn, still a small burn, tinkled by our dusty clod-hoppers' boots.

We never found that poor, lost, mad dreamer. His river-polished skeleton was discovered five months later, jammed under a rock beneath the silken waters of the Spey, but I remember him with nostalgia for he shared with me that warm thyme- and heather-scented summer long ago, when I could lie on my back yet imagine myself as one with the eagle which wheeled in the sky above my eyes, and when I had such a superabundance of energy that I felt as if I could career down the mountain slopes like the deer that fled before me.

As we sat and ate and basked a strange figure toiled up the narrow glen towards us. He was kilted with the McKenzie tartan, beneath his mouth a faded red beard hung, not unlike the pine-marten sporran which dangled from his waist. He greeted us with the polite courtesy and gentleness which is so characteristic of the islanders and highlanders – they can afford to be like that for they have proved to be savage and fearsome fighters when necessary. He had the high, chanting accent of his people, of those who have only recently learned English and still have the Gaelic as their mother tongue. He accepted some of our lunch and when he had eaten it, in repayment, he unravelled his bagpipes and began to play. The Scots amongst us affected the glassy-eyed gaze of ecstasy which they always assume when their pipes are played: the Irish, Welsh, English and Colonials donned their normal expressions of pained resignation.

He finished strangling his chanter, his drones moaned their final death-rattle and the glen echoed to the last exultant wail. We were able to tell the wandering player that we had been talking about the insistence of our hosts, the monks, on the existence of Nessie.

"Nessie lives," he replied, "and I know what she is, for I have seen her often. Each time that I have seen her she has been visible as a growing number of humps. Now, I have seen exactly the same thing in my fish farm, when an eel has got into one of the rearing ponds. When the eel swims to the surface and then wants to go down, it has to turn on its side and the undulations of its body make humps in the water just like the ones I've seen made by Nessie. Most people think of a young eel as one of those elvers they see wriggling through the wet grass towards the nearest pond, about 3 to 6 inches long, but a true baby eel is a larva, of an oval shape like a willow leaf and only about a quarter to two inches, dependent on its age, and so thin that you can see through it. All Atlantic eels, whether they are from the Thames, the Shannon, the Seine, the Rhine, the Elbe or the Sogne Fjord, originate from a vast abyss below the seaweed blanket of the Sargasso Sea. It takes them up to three years to wriggle along the currents of the Gulf Stream to Europe and then, as elvers, up brooks and burns and finally through moorland or farmland to ponds and tarns; there to reside for perhaps ten years until the urge to breed and migrate takes them back to the abyss where they were born."

The piper quaffed from a bottle of Tizer, squeezed his beard dry, and continued.

"Now, those larvae average about an inch in length, and they grow into eels whose maximum length is about four feet, but there are also in the Sargasso Sea larvae about three feet long. No one has seen the adults of these but if normal eels are about fifty times longer than their larvae that suggests the big larvae ought to grow into adults 150 feet long: sea-serpents, and Nessies."

His fish farm was only a half-hour walk downhill from the place where we had met him so we all went back with him to see it. It was surprisingly efficient and modern: a large, air-conditioned building which was a combined laboratory, hatchery and nursery, and a chain of ponds, all fed by a small burn which emptied its flow into each pond through a collection of channels and sluices. No water went from one pond to another because of the risk of transferring disease and all outlet pipes emptied back into the burn below the bottom pond. We were introduced to his three employees: his sons, all graduates of St Andrew's University. They spent part of their time experimenting with complicated genetic engineering, part in the more mundane work of feeding the stock and the rest in wooing the girls all up the glen as far as Inverness. They showed us the whole process of salmon farming from beginning to end: milking the cock salmon into a pail, the "milt" then being mixed with the hen's roe; the fertilised eggs being hatched under immaculately sterile conditions – nevertheless we saw a horrid collection of freaks which they had collected, most of them Siamese twins with double heads and double tails.

The young fish develop through a sequence of stages from parr, which are about 8 inches long, to smolts, which, in the wild, usually live in river estuaries, growing acclimatised to saline conditions, and then finally to fully grown fish, moving off to spend most of their lives in the North Atlantic until, finally, their instinct sends them back to the rivers of their infancy, there to breed and to die.

The piper and his sons reared the fish for anglers. Conventional fishing has never attracted me but I find the tackle fascinating. As a boy, I always thought that the gun-room was the most interesting room in my parents' house. I would pry around as Monk sat by the old scrubbed table fiddling about with cleaning rods and bunches of tow, yellow and harsh like the hair of Maud the Bawd, the business-woman who lived near the American aerodrome. Beside him, in the gun-case, were the armaments: a little single-barrelled .410 with which my grandfather, his son, his grandsons and his great-grandsons have learned to shoot; my 16 bore by Radcliffe of Colchester and Sam's 20 bore: a hammer-lock 10 bore, its brown barrels showing the rings of Damascus steel, it was last used by my Great-Aunt Min in about 1890; a pair of Cogswell & Harrisons made in that same year – Sam and I were given one each on our eighteenth birthdays and they are still our regular guns for filling the stew-pots; and my father's superb pair of Boss. He was convinced that Boss is the best of all gunsmiths, but Purdy or Holland & Holland also have their adherents. When my father grew older, he was lief to use the last shotgun in the case, a cheap Spanish under-and-over. Its barrels are six inches shorter than those of the Boss and it is about two pounds lighter. The other weaponry in the case were a .22 rifle, a Browning Colt .32 automatic, a Luger and my grandfather's sword.

The ammunition was kept in a large, square magazine which looked like a leather trunk. When opened it showed rows of little compartments which could be adjusted in size to fit the bore and length of the cartridges.

In an old Jacobean cupboard lay the fishing tackle, most of it made between 1870 and 1920. Here were bundles of rods, made of split cane and spliced together; reels of different sizes, some as big as soup plates and wooden, others smaller and in metal – when revolved they clattered or purred in a most pleasing manner. There were yellowing envelopes of oilcloth or parchment containing coils of line, some of transparent gut, some plaited from strands of silk and made so that they tapered as they went towards the hook; and boxes holding floats of different colours and shapes, like miniature buoys. Landing nets and gaffs hung from hooks. Most interesting of all were the leather wallets containing flies: large, brilliant salmon flies made from the feathers of exotic birds, such as the Alexander, glinting green with peacock's plumage, and smaller flies with strange names like those of moths: Blue Moit, Bracken Clock, Moor Game Brown, Snipe Bloe and Ramsbottom's Favourite.

I had to take up fishing because of my work. When I left Cambridge and began my business career the firm I joined was extremely old-fashioned. It had been founded and then run by my family who held the traditional views of many of the low-church capitalists: of the chocolate-making Quakers of Norfolk, the Methodist potters of Staffordshire and the Calvinists and Wesleyans of cotton Lancashire and wool Yorkshire. Two of these out-dated views were that in any business the leading participants, the owners, the employees and the customers, were of equal importance and secondly that any management should have worked on the factory floor. Now, of course, thanks to the combined efforts of the Harvard Business School and the Trades Union Council, British industry knows better.

In my youth, therefore, I started off as a spinner, then a weaver, then a dyer. I still think that one of the most exhilarating of noises is the thunderous roar of an old-fashioned weaving shed in full production: "old-fashioned", for looms nowadays rarely have the racketing, clacketing shuttles. As an old weaver said to me, "The weft is now either farted or peed across the warp by these new-fangled air or water jet looms."

In Halstead, our local town, almost a third of the working population were once weavers and, regrettably, the management did not realise that the noise deafened the employees (my father was as deaf as an adder because of his three years as a weaver). As a result, many people could lip-read, and it was inadvisable to gossip about anyone in the High Street if they were within eyesight.

After weaving for over 150 years, the mill was murdered in 1982. Now we can all hear.

Having woven and spun and dyed and then completed a year as a work study officer, I was sent off as a salesman of fibres and yarns to the Yorkshire worsted and woollen trades. In those days, the early 1960s, many of the proud old mills were still working flat out; it was a pleasure to visit them and smell the thick, greasy aroma of fleeces and machine oil and hear the clatter of looms or the whine of spinning frames or the whooshing of cards and combs and condensers.

The mill of Ephraim Cragthorn & Son was typical. My boss showed me the site of the mill on his street map of Huddersfield: "They're makers of fine worsted men's suiting; top quality, do quite a lot of exporting to America, Japan and Italy; a bit ashamed of using our stuff, they blend it with wool for some of their cheaper lines. The customer's name is Silas, he's the grandson of the founder; take him this new price list, he'll scream like hell, we've put everything up by five per cent."

The mill was like a stone battleship moored alongside the cobbled, grey back street, its great walls rising sheer above me, two lofty chimneys puffing out banners of coal-black smoke, the rumble and hum of engines audible through the rows of half-open windows. Under the entrance arch a Rolls Royce and a TR 2 were parked and a line of shivering salesmen, their huge cases bulging with wool samples, stood in the snow by the reception window. I joined the forlorn queue and after an hour and a half was able to ask the receptionist if I could see Mr Cragthorn.

"He's expecting you, your boss rang to say you'll be round, follow Fred here and he'll take you to him."

My first sight of Cragthorn was a scrawny pair of legs in filthy overalls sticking out from the bottom of a loom. When he had wormed his way out he proved to be an ancient, wrinkled little man with an oil-stained face and ill-fitting false teeth which snapped and slithered about his mouth when he spoke; they looked as if they were struggling to leap out of his face in order to bite me.

He nodded curtly, chucked the spanner he was holding into a toolbox and merely said, "Follow."

In his panelled office a crackling fire faced a massive desk. The walls were covered with photographs of sheep and Victorian ancestors, some of the latter being so heavily covered with beards and whiskers that they looked as if they could yield as much wool as the former. There were rows of certificates, awards and medals going back to the Great Exhibition of 1851 and the Paris Exhibition of Napoleon III. In pride of place above the hearth was an ornately scrolled, inscribed and framed tract in which some previous Cragthorn was recorded as promising total abstinence from alcohol for eternity.

A tall, svelte youth in an immaculate suit rose from an armchair next to the fire: an iced gin and tonic tinkled in his hand.

"My son, Mungo," said Silas, without much enthusiasm, and plonked himself behind the desk. "What's tha want, then?"

"I'm afraid I have to tell you that we are having to raise our prices slightly."

"We are expecting that," said Mungo affably, "you've kept them down for quite a long while."

The old man's lips snatched at his escaping teeth. He shot a glance of freezing scorn at his son and snapped, "Don't listen to the daft bugger. We'll not pay more. We'll get that artificial muck you make from the Japs, instead.'

It all ended reasonably amiably, and as time passed by we became friends. Eventually, one day, the Cragthorns asked me if I would like to go with them and fish for trout on their stretch of river. I was inclined to refuse, but my boss told me to accept: "It will be an excellent way of getting on good terms with one of our most important customers. You'll go, and you'll enjoy it, whether you like it or not."

Dominie and I happened to stay in my parents' house on the weekend before I was to fish, so I rummaged about in the old gun-room cabinet to find some tackle. Monk was on holiday. I was unable to ask his advice.

"I'm not exactly sure if I've brought all the right things," I said to old Silas, as I met him and Mungo on the river bank, a few days later.

"Well then, let's see what thee's got," said Silas, gazing with a rather rum expression at the large wooden reel which had fallen out of my carpet bag.

I proudly drew out several lengths of rod, mahogany-coloured and with fittings of brass. With a great deal of squeaking, the sections were screwed together. When united, they formed a massive pole sixteen foot along.

Silas looked glumly at it. "Taken up caber throwing, hast thou then, lad?"

Mungo gazed at it with what I took to be admiration. "It's a roach rod," he said.

"Was Roach a good maker?" I asked.

For some reason, they made no reply. In silence, they watched me fit on the reel, bind on the champagne cork which I was using as a float, and open a battered tin. It depicted, on its lid, the portraits of various aggressive women with huge hats around whom were written the words: "Women's Social and Political Union. Votes for Women. 1903."

Without saying a word, Silas Cragthorn took the tin from me and looked inside. He handed it back. He looked at his son. He spoke.

"He's got his worms in that," he said sadly.

I put a worm on my hook, tossed it in the water, felt a tug, heaved at the rod, and wound in a large fish.

"Gosh, this is fun," I said with spurious keenness. "What sort of fish is that?"

. . . . 'it's a bloody great trout' . . .

"It's a bloody great trout, that's what that is, the biggest I've bloody well seen," snarled my host. "I'm going home, I can't stand the injustice of it."

I do not know what he meant. We are still good friends, but I feel a bit hurt that he has not asked me to fish again. Perhaps he realised that I thought it a bit boring.

I was reminded of all this fishing lore and my limited experience when Mr Whippletree dropped in one day to inspect a mare who had gone off her food, and simultaneously to leave his bill. I opened it and rocked on my heels. "We had a huge bill from Fleames the millers yesterday, another from Mr Dewbit, and now this. We must find an extra way of making money to pay for this non-stop stream of bills."

"Have you ever thought of rearing fish?" asked Mr Whippletree. "I was talking to that fellow Rufus and he told me that the water meadows below his caravan site are ideal for fish farming."

"What does he know about it?"

"He seems to be a know-all about everything, but in this case I understand that he organised a form project investigating fish farming when he was a schoolmaster. I'm going there now – one of his women has sent a panicky message about her rabbit; I'll give you a lift in my van if you want."

When we arrived, the only person visible was Millicent. She was holding her rabbit between her knees, one hand grasped its scut, the thumb of the other was planted immediately below. The rabbit was struggling mightily, its normally bland features were convulsed with astonished indignation.

"Poor Nibbles," gasped Millicent. "I noticed This Huge Pink Growth on her Bottom, it seems to be Painful when she sits down. I've done what Rufus told me to do, Mr Whippletree; he said it's probably an Inverted Colon, and I should try to Push it Back with the Flat of my Thumb."

She redoubled her efforts, the rabbit bared its teeth in rage and pain.

The vet took the animal from her and inspected its behind in silence.

Finally he diagnosed: "Madam," he said, "Nibbles is merely a very well-endowed buck. You've been trying to force his testicles up his fundament."

Rufus wandered down the steps of the caravan.

"Greetings, friends," he said languidly. I explained the purpose of my visit and we all walked down the woodside hedge towards the water meadows. Rufus spread out his arms to take in the whole scene: "Here you have about fourteen acres, flat as a pancake with a stream running alongside the whole length. All you need to do is to bank up three or four ponds of about three and a half acres each and about four feet deep. Then get some young fingerling carp, preferably mirror carp, and after three years you ought to have saleable fish of around two pounds."

"Isn't four feet a bit shallow?" I asked.

"No, they don't feed if the water is too cold, and at that depth it heats up quickly in the spring: also they graze, like cows, so that you must not blanket any bottom-growing weeds from the sun."

It seemed quite a good idea, particularly as it did not involve the use of hugely expensive tanks which are used by many trout farmers; a friend of mine bought £50,000 worth and they floated down his river during a winter flood. I knew nothing of marketing fish, however, so I asked Roy Pedersen about it when we next went on his trawler.

We used to hire this trawler a couple of times a year. It was a little blunt-nosed Brightlingsea craft, with a small wheelhouse on deck, bunks for four below, and a bucket on a rope which served as the loo. An ancient engine used to potter us out into the North Sea, while a rust-red sail mouldered on the boom in case the engine failed. There was usually a crew of two, Roy and a mate, and up to twelve of us including my parents, Monk and his son, and an assortment of friends. Monk would go all nautical and nostalgic, remembering his days afloat as a petty officer during the war, and he would stand in the bows, gazing out to sea and deliberately crinkling his eyes into a weather-beaten look whilst snuffling meaningfully at the changes of breeze, and peering about for U-boats. Barely noticeable was his irritated chagrin against his small son who, behind him, knelt at the gunwales and silently but ceaselessly sicked into the sea.

We used to do about six trawls of an hour each. The moment of truth would come when the net was winched alongside, hoisted into the air and over the ship and then, as the end of the codpiece was untied, disgorged its flapping contents on to the deck. The women, having taken one curious look at the tangled mass of fish, weed, squids, shells, jellyfish and crabs, would retire into a bunched, defensive position on the stern, where they would then nitter with alarm as the crabs swarmed towards them, tiny pincers agape and eyes bulging. The men would surround the heap, pick up the trash and toss it overboard to the waiting gulls, and give the fish to Monk or Roy who would then gut and crate them. Most of the fish we caught were bottom feeders: dabs, flounders, sole and skate, but we had the occasional bonus of bass, cod, whiting and sometimes lobsters.

(It was lobsters which made my father realise how tough some of the coastal fishermen are. When he was a youth he used to go trawling with Roy's grandfather. One blustery day they trawled up a dead woman. Three lobsters fell out of the body. "I suppose we must go and tell the police or coast-guards," my father said. "No, no, boi," replied the level-headed old tar, "she's fit for another dozen lobsters. We'll set her again.")

Roy was somewhat scornful of any idea of marketing carp, but he was naturally biased against any freshwater fish, considering them as mere playthings for anglers.

"Horrible, tasteless things, carp," he said, as he sliced open a flounder with his hooked clasp-knife, and with a few deft movements gutted it, threw its corpse in a crate, its liver in a bucket and its offal overboard. "Only three sorts of people buy carp: immigrants from central Europe, like Poles, they eat carp instead of turkey at Christmas; people of the Jewish persuasion, as carp can be transferred alive for two or three days and can then be koshered; and Japanese restaurant chefs, who I'm told slice them up, squeeze lemon on them, and eat them alive."

I need not have bothered with these investigations. When I arrived home that evening I found Dominie, who hates trawling and had made an excuse not to come, bobbing up and down with excitement. "Those water meadows, they're perfect," she exclaimed with delight, as I proudly plonked three stone of crated fish on the kitchen table.

"Perfect for what? They haven't been used for ages. Bradawl mended the sluice gate last month and flooded them for the first time in thirty years."

"I know," enthused Dominie, "and now that the floods have

gone down the grass is ideal. I'll probably be able to graze ten more ponies there."

She does.

CHAPTER 9

A Bow at Another Venture

They are wet with the showers of the mountains,
and embrace the rock for want of a shelter.

Job 24 viii

My father summoned me to his panelled room which smelt of log fires and cigarettes and books and Madeira. He looked up at me over the two shuttles which ornament the centre of his desk.

"I'm too tired and frail to run the shoot any more, hardly any of my friends can now pick up a gun and I'm too close to the Grim Reaper to want to kill anything. You must take over."

I went to mourn about this to my accountant. I think he is slightly younger than me, but he has the avuncular smile and sympathetic bedside manner which experts assume when they are talking to a twit. His knowledge and common-sense when dealing with my affairs is so superior to mine that I become meekly incoherent in his presence, muttering ashamedly about overdrafts and apologising for the spelling mistakes in my latest letter. It was, therefore, with respectful attention that I listened to him talking about our shoot.

"Your father says you must take it over. I say you cannot afford it. You have the school fees for four children to pay – even those you cannot afford and you are having to sell things to pay them.

"The farming is going well, but most other 'money-making' schemes like fish farming and pony rearing are not exactly filling

102

the coffers. The costs of the shoot: Monk's salary, the Land–Rover, rearing game–birds, paying beaters and so forth – all add up to the sum of two more school fees per year. Your father has stopped rearing birds and so you are having fewer shooting parties. This means that the few birds left cost about £30 each when shot. You had better see your estate agent about it."

Cedric Cattermole, the estate agent, flicked a tiny speck of dust from his immaculately creased cavalry twill trousers, absent-mindedly plumped the snowy handkerchief in his breast pocket into more becomingly casual folds, discovered, with fastidious pleasure, a long, blonde hair caught up in a cuff-link and, having carefully unwound it and lowered it into an ashtray, gave his verdict: "Well, if you cannot afford your shoot, you will have to syndicate it."

"Do you mean get people to pay when they are asked to shoot here?"

"That's right. People 'take a gun' for a season; on average they pay about £1 for every bird shot, so if the bag is to be about two thousand head a year you should get an income of about £20,000 for ten guns: you won't make any profit, but you shouldn't lose any money, and you will still give employment to Monk and have a bit of shooting left to feed you and your family."

"I don't like the idea of asking people to pay for hospitality, surely there is some other way, and one which can even make money? I've heard that some foreign business-men pay a fortune for a few days' shooting."

"They're often inaccurate and dangerous shots, they complain bitterly if they think that they are not getting their full money's worth and they expect to be cosseted from their arrival in this country until their departure."

I was not convinced by his argument and went to a friend, a neighbour who was in a similar predicament, to discuss it further.

"I've got a cousin in Scotland," said Matthew, "who lives in a stately home only a bit smaller than mine" – a bland and slightly smug expression flitted over his face – "and he asks paying guests to shoot for two days and then to stay for the weekend. He makes an absolute packet."

I looked keen, and continued on the same theme: "They could shoot one day at yours, and one day at mine. Your house is big enough to take all the guns and their wives – or secretaries – and as you are still a bachelor I'll lend you Dominie to organise the cooking."

To my surprise, Dominie did not seem particularly enthusiastic about the idea. Monk was even glummer, although he saw the necessity of it all. He expounded on this doubt as we debated the subject round the kitchen table one morning: "I don't know if we'll get any beaters if we have all those strange people coming. Some of these foreigners have got some very funny ideas about shooting: they get into a great circle and then walk towards each other, blazing away at anything that moves – even at the gamekeepers."

Hart, who always comes to beat, agreed worriedly: "I've heard it said that most foreigners are rascals. I knew one once. He came and worked in the orchard for nearly a year. Ate everything. Black-haired little old boi, always smiling. Talked bloody rum. And mucky! He weren't fit to carry guts to a bear. Very partial to onions."

"Who the devil would want him to carry guts to a bear?" boomed Pamela. "I think this shooting idea is a demmed good wheeze. I'd take a gun meself."

Hart and Monk froze in horror over their mugs of tea, the stew on the stove hissed disapprovingly in the hush.

"I used to enjoy shooting when I was a gal, but in those days we 'of the fair sex' weren't expected to shoot; people know better nowadays."

Hart and Monk shifted their eyes towards each other and raised their brows in silent comment.

"Used to shoot snipe off the back of a Connemara pony when I stayed with my Uncle Basil in County Cork."

Monk's expression was a mixture of disgust and reluctant admiration.

"Never hit a thing, of course."

Monk looked relieved and allowed the admiration to quit his features.

"Tell you another thing," she said, her thick red fingers splaying over her tea-mug for warmth, "that nice little feller Cyril Penny-worth would be interested, he's been asking me if I know anywhere where he could get some shooting. You remember him? Chap from London who made a lot of money importing frocks from the Orient. He bought up the top three stallions in one day when he decided to start breeding cobs."

We remembered him: likeable, quick witted, rather small and with a perky manner which partly disguised a little shyness and a lot of determination.

"Can he shoot?" asked Monk.

"Just learned. I advised him to go to a shooting school and the chap who runs it says Pennyworth's a natural."

Matthew said, "I know someone else who'll take a gun, the syndicate he belonged to packed up last year: Major-General Sir Alfred Heavyside-Guestingthorpe."

"Old 'Click-click-fuck'," Monk whispered to me.

"Why is he called that?" I whispered back.

"He and his loader are never sober, his gun is usually empty. Aged almost ninety, can hardly stand. Terrible temper."

Pamela overheard us and interrupted defensively, "He's one of my favourite cousins. Used to be a demned good shot, before one of Jerry's bullets got him through the shoulder."

Monk looked sheepish and hastily said to me, "I know another excellent shot who would be interested, he's one of your friends."

"I can't ask my friends to pay to shoot."

"He won't mind. He knows he's always your guest at least once a season, and he told me a couple of years ago that if the shoot was ever syndicated he'd always be interested: Prince Harith Kahn."

Mrs Pipkin, who had been padding away quietly with her smoothing iron in a corner, said in a voice of hushed reverence, "The tinted gentleman! They do say he has hundreds of wives, and even more of them unmarried ones. I hardly dare look him in the eye." She tittered, then added, thoughtfully, "Still, I dare say they keeps him out of mischief."

Matthew and I agreed with Monk. We both liked Harith and also knew that as he was stationed as an aide in his country's London embassy he would find it easy to come to our part of England at short notice.

So it was that in one morning we found four potential guns. Matthew does not shoot, he wears great thick spectacles like cartwheels, but I had to, so we needed to find five more guns for our experiment. Within a week I had found three more by dropping in to see Mungo Cragthorn (who had forgiven the fishing episode) in his London office, and asking him if he'd like to take a gun on our trial day.

"Certainly," he said, "and my old father will be down south that weekend: he misses his shooting which we had to give up when we closed the mill; also we've got an important customer from Italy, Vittorio Sercella, whom I'd like to ask."

Once again I spoke to Cedric Cattermole on the subject.

"We've got eight guns, including myself, so we need two more. We shall have only one day's shooting, as it is an experiment. It will be on our land, but Matthew is putting up the guns and any wives for a couple of nights. That excludes Miss Rantipole, Pennyworth and the General, who want to go back to their own houses after the shoot, and Kahn, who is staying with me. I remember you said that as estate agents you kept getting enquiries from foreign business-men about spare guns, have you any at the moment?"

"Yes," he replied with reluctance, "but God knows what they're like. We have a Belgian, Jean-Pierre Pispartout and an American, Earl Ulysses Q. Pothanger. He knows of you from his son, who apparently comes and camps on your pastures during his holidays."

"Right," I said, "collect their money and send them over."

On the chosen day, all of us, beaters and guns, assembled in the stack-yard behind my parents' house. As I drove Harith and myself there from my own house I saw that the sun was already melting the frosted hedges into shattered rainbows. Plumes of breath curled about the scarlet cheeks and noses of the beaters as they chattered together, rubbing their mittened hands and stamping the hard ground with their boots. Dogs wove excited trails through the bleached grass as they investigated the new scents of the day or bristled up to each other on tip-paws. The metallic "clips" and "snaps" of barrels being fitted on to stocks cracked out from a line of cars where the guests exchanged reminiscences and hip-flasks. Monk looked immaculate in his Norfolk jacket, with his gaitered legs obscured by a ripple of labradors, his beady eyes peering beneath the brim of an old green trilby. They peered with particular beadiness at the American, Mr Pothanger, who had arranged his portly frame in a be-zippered tartan jacket which had so many pockets, patches, belts, straps and toggles that its original shape was indiscernible. Monk's eyes finally focused broodingly on a scarlet cap which surmounted this tailor's nightmare, and remained glued upon it as Matthew introduced his house party. I could only tell that Monk was hearing the introductions by the almost imperceptible fossilisation of his features: the transformation of his normal graven teak into sculptured stone.

Cragthorn and son seemed to cause Monk no undue concern, but their guest, Signor Sercella, blanched Monk into a pasty grey with disapproval. As Hart said later, "The Italian was wunnerful rum, more like a cow turd stuck with primroses." It was mainly his clothes: he was dressed entirely in brownish-maroon and yellow. His jacket was of maroon mohair, its suede shoulder patches and belt were dyed yellow to match his suede high boots, into which were tucked the bottoms of his maroon plus-fours; a yellow satin tie disappeared into the depths of a yellow and maroon checked waistcoat, of the same check as his deerstalker, which was set jauntily aslant crisp, dark curls, and had a bow of yellow satin. His trigger finger, long and slim with an almond-shaped nail, was bared to the elements; the remainder of his hands were enveloped in tight, yellow kid gloves. He made no move as we were introduced, just a quick glance from huge, lustreless brown eyes, like those of a dead calf, and a couple of moues and a pout. He kept pouting which drew attention to his lips: they were almost circular, thick and rather bluish, the last time I had seen anything like them was when I had to take the temperature of a foal.

The Belgian seemed little better, for, although his clothing was reasonably conventional and designed to blend with Mother Nature's complexion, he was handling his gun, which he had already loaded, as if it were a conductor's baton.

"Excusay moi, monsewer," said Monk, flinching as the barrels pointed straight into his face for the tenth time, "but avez-vous any experience des shooting before?"

"But of course! I am often shooting the birds as they sing in the trees: the lark, the blackbird and the chiff-chaff. I make the chase of them often and with frequency." He then pointed his gun at my father's weather-cock and shouted "Pam! Pam!" laughing heartily as he did so.

"Earl Ulysses Q. Pothanger," continued Matthew glumly.

"Cor, that fat little bloke's a nobleman," stage-whispered a beater.

A grinding rattle interrupted and an ancient Mini doddered into the yard. In it sat Major-General Sir Alfred Heavyside-

Guestingthorpe and his loader. Pamela had told me that these two had been in the army together: the loader had been the general's soldier-servant for several decades and in most parts of the world.

The old warrior had difficulty getting out.

"Goddammit, open the door wider!" he bellowed.

"I'm a-trying to, sir, damn me if I ain't!" yelled his loader.

"Well, try harder, you idle dotard!"

"Do you try harder, you silly old fool, sir. You're so stiff you've seized up!"

With an excess of grunting, pulling and heaving, which reminded me of a shrimp trying to evict a hermit crab from its shell, our guest was finally extricated, and he and his loader tottered over to us. A strong smell of whisky emanated from them.

"Bless my soul!" exclaimed the General, and peered short-

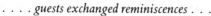

. . . . . guests exchanged reminiscences . . .

sightedly at the Italian, "what a shtrdy – extradin – extraordinary feller."

Pamela strode up and thumped him fondly on the back. "Mornin', Cousin Freddy," she boomed. "Haven't seen you since the Essex Show; let me introduce you to Cyril Pennyworth, who's staying with me."

Whilst these introductions were taking place, Harith had strolled up to Monk.

"Hello, Monk, old bean!" he shouted breezily. "Are you giving us a wizard lot of birds today, what?"

"I hope so, your Highness, but I don't know what with the rains during the nesting season and the poachers nowadays being what they are and I've never seen so many stoats and weasels about wild cats are even worse and then Mr Wright's new combine is even more destructive and of course these ponies keep trampling

. . . . 'Hello, Monk, old bean!' . . .

on eggs and if I've said once I've said a hundred times . . ." His plaint was interrupted by Harith, who knows the speech of keepers.

"Last time I am shootin', Monk old bean, it is at tigers."

Monk looked unimpressed. "Well, you'll not find any here, this is a well-kept shoot."

Pothanger came up to me, trembling with fastidious indignation.

"Your bird-dog has just committed an act of personal hygiene against my gun case," he fumed.

Mungo hissed over his shoulder, "For God's sake get that senile old soldier and his loader away from my best customer; they keep telling poor Vittorio how many Italians they captured in the desert."

Monk and I hastily mobilised the beaters and guns, the former drifting under the gamekeeper's direction to line up on the nearside of the wood which lies adjacent to the stack-yard, the latter climbing into a tractor-drawn trailer and settling down on the straw-bales which Tony Crisp had furnished as seats. We departed in a fine hail of frozen slush and mud which showered from the tractor tyres and besprinkled the two guns nearest to the front. Pennyworth was one of them but his annoyance changed to amusement as he saw the expression of his fellow sufferer: "Cheer up, signor, you look like Saint Sebastian shot froo wiv 'is 'arrers."

Matthew placed the guns in their correct positions and finally, as I rested on my shooting stick and stared into the dark green tranquil depths of the wood, I began to relax.

But not for long.

The first bird of the day must have been colour blind, or crass, or merely inquisitive, for it flew directly over the gaudily garbed Pothanger. He raised his gun. A shot rang out; then another; then, to our united astonishment, another; a fourth; another; and then two more.

He had a pump gun.

Old Cragthorn, who was placed between the American and me, cackled with ironic glee. He caught my eye as I turned to stare after the indignantly departing tail of the pheasant as it flew onwards to the next wood and said reassuringly, "Never fear, yon bird will die of nervous prostration if it doesn't die first of lead poisoning." Pothanger's gun rattled into action once again and Cragthorn's merriment changed to anger when he saw that the barrage was directed at a bird directly over his head.

"You shoot your own birds, and I'll shoot mine," he shrilled, and swinging his gun up, brought the bird down, although almost out of shot, with his first barrel.

After the drive Monk came up to me.

"Not many dead birds: I sent a good number up and heard plenty of shooting."

"Half of what you heard came from a pump gun. There's a lot of runners I'm afraid," I replied apologetically. "We seem to have only three good shots: Kahn, Pennyworth and Mungo Cragthorn; four are fair: Silas Cragthorn, the Belgian, Miss Rantipole and myself; and three bad: the old General, Sercella and Pothanger."

"Odd that the Belgian isn't too bad," said Matthew.

"Probably because he's used to shooting tiny little fast birds. However, he is bloody dangerous. Thank God he hasn't got the pump gun."

During the next drive the American's fusillades eventually brought down a bird and I overheard him talking to Bradawl, who was leaning on a stick, his wig pulled down well over his ears to keep off the nippy breeze, a sack tied round his waist like an apron to keep off the dew.

"I have displaced a pheasant from its aerial environment and am not fully ascertained of its present whereabouts."

"Is it dead?"

"Its existence is not entirely terminated, but it exhibited strong symptoms of a negative health reaction."

"Cock or hen?"

The portly colonial hesitated. "Its gender was masculine."

"Has anyone seen the American gentleman's cock?" bawled Bradawl.

"Yes!" bawled another beater, who turned to re-holler down the hedge: "Hey, Ted, that running cock you saw belonged to the American."

"But he's got it in his hand."

"No, Ted, that's too little; he's picked up someone else's cock; he got an older and larger one."

"I seen his little old cock tower and then drop," shouted another. "It's one of those melanistic sorts: a great big black 'un."

"Here it is!" shouted a small boy with a large retriever. "Tell him my Sniffles has found his cock caught up in this here bush."

Mr Pothanger collected his bird, rather grumpily, the small boy thought, and then joined the rest of us by the trailer.

As we talked, mainly about our prowesses during the last drive, Pamela noticed Signor Sercella standing in a graceful pose with one hand lying elegantly athwart a small knife which hung in a maroon sheath of embossed suede from his belt.

"What do you use that for?" she barked.

The Italian's eyes lit upon her pork-pie hat, travelled dubiously down her tweeded form and stopped, puzzled, on the heavy green skirt which swung, like a large lampshade, above her boots.

"The signor is a priest?" he asked.

"The signor is a signorina," she guffawed in return.

Sercella raised an eyebrow in silent comment and then returned to her original question. "This knife is used for the opening of the veins."

"Whose veins?" asked the stalwart Amazon, uneasily. "Do you have some sort of blood feud?"

"No, it is the veins of the beasts I kill. I do not normally shoot these little birds and rabbits and other baby things, I kill the lions, the elephants, the wildebeests and the gorillas and if they do not die at once I open their veins so . . ." and in one movement he had unsheathed his knife and whipped it across his throat.

"Damn feller, shoots poor bloody gorillas," shouted the General, moist-eyed, and was promptly reeled tactfully out of earshot by his loader.

"How do you shoot gorillas?" asked Harith.

"We get a signorina from the village when she is in her season and we tie her to a tree. The gorilla, he comes at night for her and I am up the tree, and I kill him with my .303."

A shocked silence fell over us. It was broken by Mungo Cragthorn: "What happens if you miss the gorilla?"

Sercella shrugged: "That is, what you say, 'hard cheese' for the signorina."

The wind had veered to the east during lunch. As I sat on the bleakly exposed top of Bouchers Hill Pasture I was made coldly aware that, between me and the birthplace of the wind in the Central Russian Uplands, there was nothing higher than the spire of Warsaw Cathedral sticking out of the Central Plain of Poland, some factory chimneys in Hanover, a few masts and funnels amongst the frozen canals of Holland and the ice-green waves of the North Sea. I looked down the hill slopes on either side and could tell from the huddled and motionless posture of the other guns that they felt as cold as I. Far away, amongst the clouds that loomed dark and sombre over the marshlands, thunder boomed and muttered; a spot of rain flicked my cheek, a few more random drops hit my hat with hard "plonks" and then it began to rain steadily.

I saw faces turn hopefully in my direction and then, disappointed that I made no move, look away and hunch further into upturned collars. Signor Sercella undid the satin bow of his deerstalker and tied it beneath his chin. Monsieur Pispartout produced a minute packet from a pocket which, when unwrapped and donned, proved to be a transparent cape of thin plastic. Mr Pothanger fussed about his jacket as if he were a one-man wrestling bout and it sprouted a couple of extensions like shirt tails, a hood, and some knitted tubes which crept out of his sleeves, along his wrists and up the backs of his hands. Pamela got off her shooting-stick, up-ended it, pressed a button and it blossomed into a large green umbrella. The rest of the party sat in sullen silence except for the General and his loader who seemed to be searching for, and arguing about, a missing hip-flask.

The rain continued to teem. A melancholy wail floated along the valley: Monk's horn indicating that the beaters had reached their starting point. The small, wizened figure of the gun on my left, Silas Cragthorn, hopped off his shooting-stick and stumped towards me.

"Here, lad," he cried, "the beaters have only just begun. How long is this drive likely to last?"

"About another three-quarters of an hour," I said.

"I'm now old enough to do as I will, and my will at this moment is to get out of this bloody awful weather. I'm going back to the trailer: there's a barn next to it where you'll find me when the drive's over."

Off he plodded and George, who had been acting as a back gun to shoot any winged flyers – an unfortunately large number of them, that day – moved up to take his place.

A pony's head appeared over the crest of the hill and stared at us. It was Bumble Bee. His inquisitive face was joined by a row of others: the rest of his herd. Mr Pothanger was the main object of their attention, probably because of his weird shape. Finally their curiosity overcame their shyness and, led by the stallion, they trotted down the hill and gathered round him in a circle, gazing at him with friendly but critical eyes. Mr Pothanger grew uneasy under this battery of stares and suddenly waved his arms.

"Absent yourself from my proximity," he ordered. The ponies pricked their ears in unison, looked wonderingly at each other, then back at him. Bumble Bee edged closer, very stealthily stretched out his neck and head, and extending his long upper lip used it to grasp the end of Mr Pothanger's tartan sleeve. Mr Pothanger rose from his shooting-stick with alarm, but just then a bird flew over me and at the noise of my shot the ponies scampered off, to take up position once more peering over the crest of the hill.

We waited on. The wind freshened and the rain changed its angle of entry and attacked us almost horizontally, so that it was like a swarm of snow-bees aimed directly at my nape which was exposed below the dripping and shapeless brim of my trilby. A lone pheasant squelched above M. Pispartout but he did not notice it: he was staring miserably at his feet. The rumbling of thunder became louder and more ominous. Pothanger suddenly made off towards the trailer at a galumping canter; Pennyworth and Sercella followed him; the remaining stoics moved closer together towards the central position. In a way I was grateful to the departing guns as I was able to leave my hill-top, where I had no wish to be if the incoming thunder was to be accompanied by lightning.

It was an unproductive drive, the few pheasants which flew were mainly sent up by a fox, and because of the rain they plunged down as soon as they could into the beech hedge which fronted the wood; they were finally sent up in one flush by the disobedient spaniel of a beater, running too far forward, and they flew back over the wood. When the beaters finally reached the end of the drive and burst through the hedge their expressions of chagrin and disgust at finding barely half the guns in position were somewhat humiliating, of greater humiliation was what happened next.

A lone partridge flew alongside the hedge, very low and in front of the beaters.

M. Pispartout's gun rose.

"Pam!" it said.

"Bloody hell!" shrieked a beater, slapping his hand to a bleeding earlobe.

Ignoring the lamentations filling the air from the stricken beater, M. Pispartout's gun spoke again.

"Pam!"

"He's got me," shouted another beater, excitedly looking down and searching frantically through his trousers.

The partridge flew on. M. Pispartout began re-loading.

"No!" we all screamed: guns, beaters, labradors and onlooking ponies.

M. Pispartout looked around resentfully, "But I have not shot anything this drive."

"That's what he thinks," said Monk, running up, panting. "I think we should end the day. They're not badly hurt but they're bloody angry. We'll have to pay compensation."

We arrived home, crestfallen and rain-sodden. Dominie and the wives were sitting in front of the fire, looking decorative. Apart from Dominie, the most ornamental was Madame Pispartout, a svelte brunette with scarlet lips and a long cigarette-holder.

"Your husband has just shot a beater," I panted angrily, drawing up to a stop in front of her.

She removed the cigarette-holder from her lips, gazed at me under lids heavy and sultry with mascara and smiled in a kind but condescending manner.

"How ver' interesting, you must show it to me sometime," she drawled, and proceeded to eat a muffin.

"Well, we're not doing that again," I said, after we had finished some calculations. "It cost a fortune to appease those shot beaters, and the time and worry has in no way been compensated for by the income we got."

"I don't know," replied Dominie, "I sold two ponies to Mrs Pothanger: they have a Welsh Mountain Pony stud in Maine."

I have told Dominie that she can no longer expect to sell ponies at shooting parties, we have syndicated the shoot and it is now full of safe – but sensible – local friends.

CHAPTER 10

Driving

The driving is like the driving of Jehu,
the son of Nimshi; for he driveth furiously.
                                    II Kings 9 ii

I had a Great-Uncle who was greatly admired locally for his
three hobbies: washing his maidservants in his farmyard trough,
drinking, and driving a tandem. His wife, in her day, was said to
have "the finest figure of a girl on a horse in all of Ireland", but I
remember her chiefly for her strange custom of shaving off her
eyebrows and replacing them with pencilled substitutes halfway
up her forehead, thus giving herself an expression of alarmed
surprise. She disliked my Great-Uncle's hobbies, thinking the first
uncouth, the second unhealthy and the third unsafe. She was
correct to fret about his tandem driving, for a tandem was the
horsedrawn equivalent of a motor-bicycle, fast and dangerous. My
parents' cook, Sophie, who shared my Great-Aunt's disapproval,
said that as a girl she had always been warned by those who had
the safety and decorum of young virgins at heart: "Never go in a
tandem with a young man nor up in a balloon with Sir Cxxx de
Cxxxx." The latter died old and respected, having earned fame
for two remarkable achievements: winning the high-diving competition at Southend when in his eighties, and being the subject of a
whole chapter (entitled the "Amateur Hangman") in the most
authoritative book on sexual perversions. My Great-Uncle, on
the other hand, died young, as a result of lying blotto in a damp

116

ditch all night with the remains of his tandem on top of him.

Actually a tandem is a method of harnessing, not a vehicle. Two horses are involved, one in front of the other, Indian file. The vehicle is normally a two-wheeler, not too light and perhaps a bit wider than usual as it is apt to undergo more erratic movements, particularly if the lead horse decides to double back on its tracks or to get a rear leg caught over one of the traces. Tandem driving earned its reputation because of the "young bloods", mainly cavalry officers, who took it up as a competitive sport in the relaxed and heady days after the Crimean War; but there were many women drivers. I have an article written by Lady Georgiana Curzon in 1889 who says scathingly:

We are often told that a tandem is the most dangerous mode of conveyance ever invented by the human mind . . . . I admit that these criticisms have a certain amount of truth in them, especially if those who speak are afflicted with that unfortunate complaint, "want of nerve".

But they bred women and horses tough in those days.

My parents had a much less exciting conveyance, a governess-cart: a roundish tub on wheels with a little cast-iron step at the back, a tiny door which let one enter the seating area, and a pair of two-seater pews facing each other; there was no forward-facing seat so the driver had to sit awry in the front of the offside pew. Apart from taking me out for reluctant inhalations of fresh air the main job of my pony Polly was to pull this trap. In those far-off days, just after the war, petrol had not only reached the dizzy price of about a shilling a gallon, but it was also rationed; and so it was that my mother used to go shopping in the cart. I still vividly remember the clippety-clop of hooves, the creak of harness, the gritty crunching of the tyres, the rattle of beer crates, the sour smell of horse and the sweet smell of hedgerow, the fat behind of the pony between the shafts, my mother's gloved hands holding the reins, the knobbles on the polished holly-stick whip, and, in the lane behind, the lolling red tongue and one-ear-up-and-one-ear-down of Rags as he disobeyed orders to stay at home.

The baker and the butcher both delivered in traps, and coal was lugged around the villages by a tired, shaggy horse of unknown type. Many of the older people knew how to ride, many of the middle-classes still spent more time being transported by horse or pony than by machine.

We had cart horses on the estate, Suffolk Punches, like great copper-coloured barrels trundling over the hedgy landscape as they pulled ploughs or two-wheeled tumbrils or four-wheeled waggons. There were two types of waggon, the first nicknamed after the hard-working immigrants who came here in droves to earn their living between the wars, the Scotch Barge; the second waggon being our local speciality, designed to take our huge harvests of corn, the Essex Large Waggon. I always thought that these looked rather unsafe, for the front wheels seemed disproportionately small, partly because the fore end of the waggon reared up higher than the back and partly because the back wheels were so large, exactly the same height as Bell, our woodman: five foot, nine inches. I remember the conflicting emotions of comfort, curiosity and cowardice when we children lay on the top of a load of harvested sheaves, swaying just below the heavy branches of the hedgerow oaks and elms and seeing the backs of the Punches straining at the harness far below. Most of the horses were used by the smaller farmers, like old Howlett who could be seen, many evenings, sitting on Dodman's back, which he had upholstered with a bit of sacking. He sat side-saddle, as if he were on a sofa, smoking a pipe and gazing into the distance. Occasionally he'd tap his wife with a hazel wand as she puttered along on her corned feet below him, to tell her to get a move on. I regret that in those days I had more admiration for the machinery of the larger farmers, particularly and most impressively of all, for the converted Sherman Tank that Mr Wright used to pull his plough during the spartan years of Attlee's rule.

The kings of any parish or farm were the horsemen. They dressed differently from the average farm labourer; often with gypsy-like moleskin trousers, patent leather collars and billy-cock hats – Hart told me that before the war they often decorated these hats with feathers. Like many "mysteries" – groups of people in a trade or occupation – the horsemen formed cliques which were a cross between a modern trades union, an ancient guild and a religious society; these were given esoteric names like "The Toadmen" of Ely and "The Horseman's Word" in Morayshire, and like many secret societies they had a set sequence of ritual which took place during the initiation of new recruits.

. . . . he sat side-saddle . . .

First, there was the Introduction: the initiates, young men (women were never admitted), were assembled in a group, the number of which had to be odd, preferably thirteen. This grouping took place on a special date, usually around Martinmas (in November), and in an isolated building, generally a barn. This they entered by means of special signs: passwords, numbered rappings and so forth. They were then interrogated by the "ministers" on such subjects as their motive for joining and their rights and claims to admission.

Second, came the Instruction: the passing of trade secrets and information, these included a potted history which started with the first horseman, and tips and charms. The most important charm of all was "The Word", the use of which would freeze a horse in its tracks.

The Confirmation came third: a ritual which involved the welcoming benison and the promise from the initiates that they would keep The Word secret, "neither to dite, write nor recite it".

Finally, there was a Celebrationary Feast. This often ended with a toast shouted or sung in a merrily drunken manner:

> Here's to the horse with the four white feet,
> The chestnut mane and tail,
> A star on his face and a spot on his breast,
> And his master's name was CAIN.

The best horseman on our land was Amos Quartermain. (Rider Haggard was staying in our village whilst writing one of his books: he may have called his hero Allan Quartermain after Amos' family.) Amos could plough the straightest furrow and had the most calming of touches with all horses, even the half-hysterical hackney which used to pull the four-wheeled dog-cart driven variously by Miss Westly-Waterless, or her Italian prisoner-of-war, Lorenzo, or Rasmus, her chimpanzee, depending which was the most sober. Amos is still about, but a very old man. When he heard about Rufus' caravan and cob he asked me if I could drive him over the fields to the encampment so that he could have a look. Captain Firecrest and Hart came with us, the Captain because he happened to drop in and see us and he always likes the chance to look at a horse, Hart because he needed to collect some bean sticks from the wood, he said, but I reckon that it was to gaze with disapproving delight down Karen's décolletage.

After the horse had been inspected, the caravan admired, the bean sticks cut and the décolletage disapproved, we all sat on some bales round the fire and quaffed the tea which was always at hand. Old Amos produced a small leather bag from his pocket.

"Me charms," he explained, "me frog-bone and me colt-milt."

"Colt-milt!" exclaimed Rufus delightedly. "I've heard of that. It's a flattish oval pad the colour of liver and it lies at the back of the colt's tongue when it's in the womb. It's normally swallowed during the birth, but if you are quick enough you can hook it out of the colt's mouth with your finger. You are meant to use it as a helpful charm when breaking horses. I don't know why only colts have it, and not fillies . . ."

"It's both," snapped the old man, riled by the know-all flow of information which was obscuring his own erudition. "In these here parts we call any young horse a colt, whatever its sex."

He loosened the drawstring of the bag and riffled within, finally extracting a dirty little object which looked like a wish-bone.

"This here is the frog-bone. You burn a frog – some people say a toad but I reckon it should be a frog because horses' hooves have frogs – and cast its ashes in a brook. The thing that floats agin' the current, upstream, that's the frog-bone. You use it to stay horses in their tracks, they'll not move till you command them, whatever anyone else tries. This here bone was given me by my Great-Uncle Ben, a Whisperer."

"What is a Whisperer?" whispered Millicent to Rufus.

"Whisperers are meant to be a group of people who have learned the secrets of controlling horses by whispering certain words into their ears. Their lore is supposed to go back thousands of years and the language they use may be a remnant from the Ice Age, like the numbers which shepherds use when counting sheep."

Rufus turned to the old man. "What words do you use to control horses?"

"We've got special words in Essex and East Anglia. They use different ones to the west and yet other ones in the Shires. For 'right' we say 'wardie', but they say 'het' to the west and they say 'wheesh' in parts of Norfolk. Over the river, in Kent, they say 'gee' for 'go left', but we say 'wardie-to-the-left' or 'come-here'; in the Shires they say 'come-back'. Of course, most peoples say 'woa' and 'gee-up' for 'stop' and 'go'."

"I wouldn't be surprised if some of those weren't Celtic or pre-Celtic also," said Rufus.

We pondered at the thought.

Presently Millicent murmured, platitudinously, "You can see Faces in the Twigs and Branches of Trees or amongst the Glowing Embers of a Fire. I love looking for them."

"I don't," said Hart. "It reminds me of the night that my mum and my dad and I and my fourteen brothers and sisters were a-sitting round the great old fireplace at home and suddenly my brother Harry lets out a scream like I've never heard since. He had seen a face so terrible and so awesome amongst the flames that he'd still wake up sweating about it sixty years later."

"Whatever was it like?"

"He said that the worst of it was that it looked so ordinary, like anyone you'd meet in the lane. It was its expression as it burned that gave him the horrors."

"Your house was haunted by several ghosts, wasn't it?" I asked, leading him on.

"By three: there was the woman in the silk dress, do you look out of the window at twilight, you'd see her, just, like a thin shape moving under the apple tree, but you'd hear her dress rustle as she walked away. Then there was the cobbler who lived in the cottage afore we moved in, you could hear the 'tap-tap' of him working sometimes at nights. Then there was the slate-coloured thing."

Having hooked his audience, he paused to relight the home-rolled cigarette which drooped like a skewbald caterpillar from his lips.

"On each side of the great old kitchen fireplace there were two other little rooms, cupboards almost, for they were no deeper than the chimney stack: one was the washroom and the other was the larder. The larder door had a four-inch gap between it and the floor. One evening my sister Martha gave out a regular old screech and hollered out: 'Look! There's a serpent a-coming out from under that door!' And sure enough, when we looked, there was a long, thin, slate-coloured thing a-wriggling below the door. But it wasn't coming out, it seemed to be stuck. It made a sort of scooping motion. And my dad said, 'That's no serpent, that's a dog's paw.' And sure enough, that's what it were. So my dad picked up the poker and opened the door. And there was nothing there. Not even the paw. And my dad said that when he had taken over from the cobbler, after he had died there, he had found a slate-coloured dog shut up in the larder there. Dead."

We stayed silent, shocked. Millicent began to snivel and rocked to and fro, clutching the August-Personage-In-Jade to her bosom. Hart, gratified by our reaction, launched himself into a torrent of further stories: of the chariot-riding shape of Queen Boudicca with her death-white face and blood-red hair; of Dick Turpin on his headless horse lurking in the thickets of the forests of Epping and Hainault; of the Screaming Skull of Rushbrook Hall and the Hovering Coffin of Stisted; of Black Shuck, the devil's one-eyed hound, which lopes along the loneliest lanes and howls amid the thunderstorms; of the church bells tolling off the coast from the drowned churches in the North Sea; of the clash of swords heard in the mists by Maldon, as once again the doomed Tharl Brithnoth leads his little troop of Saxon defenders against the Viking horde of the Sea-King Anlaff; of Sharpfight Meadow in Little Cornard where once there was fought a battle between a red dragon from Essex and a black one from Suffolk; of The Dauntless Girl who feared neither man nor devil; of the wicked man from Tolleshunt d'Arcy who was so evil that he had to be buried within the churchyard wall but "the devil, he came along, and he scraped him out"; of the Green Children, discovered lost and forlorn in a field eight hundred years ago; of Mad Mehala of the Marshes and of Old Mother Redcap, the witch of Foulness Island.

"We've burnt more witches in Essex than has the rest of England put together," concluded Hart with a somewhat perverse satisfaction.

"Still, that was a long time ago," said Gloria.

"Not that long, my Uncle Albert was one of the people who helped drown poor Old Dummy, the wizard, in the brook in Sible Hedingham; that was in 1863."

"When I was a boy," I said, "there were two witches in our village. I remember most poor old Widow Shrike, she always dressed in black and was very tall and thin; she had a terrible limp and the pain in her leg made her bare her teeth so that she'd come at you snarling and we children would run in panic from her. Now that I am older I realise that she was just a poor, lonely old woman – even though a witch."

"There is always an explanation for these things," said Rufus condescendingly. "For example, those Green Children you mentioned were probably that colour because they had the 'ague', the old word for malaria, and people couldn't understand them because the locals here did not recognise a Lincolnshire or Cambridgeshire accent."

"Perhaps," agreed Hart, and then looked scornfully at Millicent's cauldron hanging over the fire. "It's said that they ate nothing but beans, perhaps it's them being vegetarianisms that they turned green."

"After we bought Hippocampus," Rufus continued, "I made a special study of the superstitions and religions associated with horses. There is an amazing amount, probably caused by the long and personal association man has had with the horse. Like the dog, the horse has been thought of as an assistant and a companion, not just a source of food. In fact, as far as food goes, the reverse has happened and the horse has become the totem, and therefore the taboo, of certain peoples, particularly the Celts of Britain. You can see the totemic pictograph still as the outlines of horses cut out of the turf: some are lost, like the one on the Gog Magog Hills near Cambridge or the Red Horse of Tysoe, but the White Horse of Uffington still exists, all 370 feet of it, looking very like the horses on some Celtic coins, and the White Horse of Westbury."

Rufus stirred the tea in his mug with a twig and continued in his most school-masterly manner, "Totems, or clan symbols, are almost always associated with taboos and we still do not eat horse flesh in this island, or mention a 'white' horse, it is always a 'grey'."

Hart interrupted, "White horses are lucky, so are horses with white stockings on their front legs. If they've got a white star on their foreheads, that's double lucky."

Captain Firecrest shook his head: "Not all white-coloured are lucky – *I looked, and behold a pale horse: and his name that sat on him was Death.*' Revelations, Chapter 7, verse viii."

Rufus looked piqued, but went on, "There are still legends of ghostly hounds and unearthly horsemen: Herne the Hunter in the old Forest of Windsor and the Yeth Hounds in Wistman's Wood in Dartmoor, for instance, or even the famous cowboy song 'Riders in the Sky', where a ghost cowboy eternally rounds up steel-hoofed cattle 'across the endless skies'.

"A related belief is the phantom battle when you can hear the clash of steel and the rumble of hooves, for example Chequers Street in St Albans which echoes a long-past battle from the Wars of the Roses, and sometimes Sedgemoor, where the troops of James, Duke of Monmouth, were slaughtered by those of King James II."

Rufus was well into his stride now.

"Legends still exist of Monster Horses, evil beasts who usually live in water – the sea, or rivers or lakes – and feed on young maidens," he went on, with relish.

"The Celts had a horse goddess, known as Epona. The Roman cavalry adopted her and there is at least one stone sculpture of her, riding side-saddle, wearing a cloak and diadem and holding the key to a stable door. The gods and goddesses of a previous religion often become the devils and demons of its successor, perhaps the Celtic goddesses became Christian witches; certainly witches sometimes are meant to use horses instead of broomsticks to travel to their coven meetings. In the early morning you can tell if your horse has been ridden by its sweat and exhaustion, and by the stringy pads on its mane called 'hag knots' which show where the witch has wound her fingers round to keep from falling off. Horses are very vulnerable to witchcraft and to the evil eye, that is why they are hung with protective amulets and charms such as brasses, though the horse brass as we know it only really came into favour around 1850. The most popular motifs include hearts, stars, sun-flashes and crescents which suggests that the gypsies, who are very fond of those designs, may have been responsible for the origin of brasses.

"Of course, horseshoes are lucky, but you must nail them on your door (Nelson had one nailed to the mast of the *Victory*) with the horns uppermost to hold the good fortune, only smiths and farriers or people called Smith can position them upside-down."

The rest of us were mesmerised by this fund of knowledge, but Hart managed to interrupt, "When I was a young man, anyone buying a motorcar tried to get one with a 'U' on its numberplate, because that represented the lucky horseshoe."

Then he changed the subject. For some time he had been watching Millicent fossicking over a small plant in a pot. "What's that you're a-tittivating?"

"It's a Dear Little Peach from a stone I planted."

"When it gets much older and has flowers, you should fertilise it with a rabbit's scut."

"The Precious One, how Horrible!"

"Not at all, all you have to do is to plunge it into the centre of one flower so that the pollen sticks to it and then lightly tickle the stamens of another flower to transfer the pollen."

"I can certainly Understand why the pollen Sticks to it, but isn't the whole Thing rather Repulsive to Hold?"

"Repulsive? Of course not: I got about six rabbits' scuts when our Beryl was a little doddymite and made her a doll out of them."

Millicent stared at Hart, speechless with nausea and amazement.

He continued, "Here, I'll give you one, I've got a spare one in my pocket."

She shrank back with a "Yeugh!" of alarm and then gawped in wonder at the fluffy object that he held out to her.

"But that is a Rabbit's Tail."

"Yes, a rabbit's scut."

"Oh! Scut! I thought you said Rabbit's Gut."

Hart stared coldly at her. "I ain't likely to make a dolly for our Beryl out of a pile of innards," he said with indignation.

I changed the subject hastily. Hart is a well-tempered man, but when he is annoyed he "gets proper riled", as he himself admits.

"We are going over to the aerodrome to a meeting of the driving club, why don't you come with us, Rufus, you've been saying that you would like a look at all the different horse and pony-drawn vehicles?"

We were standing in a shivering crowd on the wind-blasted expanse of the aerodrome.

Mrs Fewmet stiffened. "Do you mean that common-looking person in the cheap jumper and carrying those brown paper parcels is Pamela Rantipole? The *Honourable* Pamela Rantipole? The daughter of the *Earl* and *Countess* of Moistment? Whose brother, *Viscount* Pruddick, has just married *Princess* Lavicious-Leczinskya? The Moistments of Prullick *Hall*, Glenwillie *Castle* and two hundred and six *Belgrave Square*? The dear person, you must introduce me, we have so many friends in common." She beetled over to Pamela, lugging me with her.

"Pamela, this is Monique Fewmet, she owns the Whiteladies Stud." Pamela nodded cordially: "How-de-do? Heard of your stud. You're very brown, what? Just back from your hols?"

"She's been telling me about her super bungalow on the French seaside," I explained.

"My Villa On the Riviera," Monique corrected icily, then turning her back on me she continued, "Now, my dear Pamela, you and I must really get together, I've heard so much about you from the Belted-Galloways . . ."

The wind continued to blast away, whining dolefully through the struts of the vast, Second World War hangar in which we were assembled. We were the guests of Group-Captain Fingersides, a new recruit to Mr Ryan's driving club who thought, correctly, that the use of one of his empty buildings and the resources of his rarely-used perimeter runways would be useful to the club. The club was only a year old, but already consisted of over 20 members. Their conveyances ranged from home-built rattle-traps, pulled by shaggy objects which looked like animated hearth rugs, to the coach of Major and Mrs Booth, a magnificently elegant vehicle nearly a hundred years old; it holds four people within its panelled and glass walls and two others can sit on the driver's seat. It is pulled by a dapper pair of greys and is hired out for weddings.

Dominie became an enthusiastic member of the driving club, much to the gratification of Mr Kimberwick, the saddler. After she had been to his frowsty workshop to discuss the harness she wanted tailored for Bumble Bee she told me that it was as complicated as buying a wedding dress. Firstly Mr Kimberwick needed to know if she wanted the harness for the show-ring or for everyday use: for the former purpose it would have to be made of black patent leather and with a collar, but a working harness is usually of ordinary brown leather, and a breast strap can be used instead of a collar if the conveyance is not too heavy. Dominie, having decided to have an ordinary working harness, then had to decide on the leather. Mr Kimberwick proudly drew out sheaf after sheaf of different leathers: in colours from pale parchment to dark brown, in textures from soapily smooth to granular, with whorled grains or parallel grains, supple or brittle, from stomach or shoulder, Pakistani or British, elastic or taut, very expensive or very, very expensive. He is besotted about the mediums and materials of his trade; normally taciturn, he waxes eloquent on the subject. He once gave me a disgusting and therefore interesting lecture about the two so-called "Viking Skins" nailed on the front doors of a couple of local churches, after analysis he considers that one comes from the haunch of a Chamois or goat and the other from the shoulders of a human being.

Whilst Mr Kimberwick was making the harness, Bradawl made a "breaking float" to Mr Ryan's specification. It was basically a low wooden platform on a couple of wheels and with a pair of shafts, which were extra long so if Bumble Bee decided to kick he could do so without pounding the float to pieces. Dominie would sit on a straw-bale placed upon this conveyance and she and the pony would then practise the art of driving. When finally she felt proficient, she bought the cheapest chariot available: a spindly seat on a pair of thin wheels called an exercise-cart. For a few weeks Bumble Bee towed her round the lanes in this frail contraption but she found it a depressingly frightening occupation: cars and motor-bicycles rushed at her from around corners, or having overtaken her would cut in too early, causing the pony to rear back in self-defence; surly salesmen in a hurry hooted at her to get a move on; whenever she had to drive along the main road to reach the other side of our valley the wind created by overtaking juggernauts or buses buffeted her into the verge or sucked the light cart towards the centre of the road. One of the driving club members had his horse killed on the same road and Dominie reluctantly decided to give up regular driving, she found it too frightening and also it took up too much of her scarcely available time. A year later I discovered an old governess-cart in someone's barn and bought it for £30. Bradawl repaired it: all that it needed was the replacement of some worm-eaten boarding and a couple of coats of paint; fortunately the wheels were sound, for there are not many wheelwrights left and their scarce and skilled services are expensive.

We sometimes jogged out in this cart, but mainly over the pastures of the estate; even that pleasure ceased when the cart was smashed by the idiot Edwin Scatterwell, as described later. Now, the only pony-drawn conveyance we use is a costermonger's cart, bought from Pamela's London friend, Cyril Pennyworth. It is a small but solidly built four-wheeler, it has a bench in front for the driver and two friends and a board rises above and behind them upon which we have painted the name of the stud. Dominie takes it out sometimes, I have taken it out once; I spent most of the time judging which was the more disagreeable, the teeth-rattling action of the cart or the unflattering cries from school children of "Come and have a look, here's Steptoe and his nag, want any old bones, mister, he's bloody slow I prefer a moty-bike."

I prefer one also.

CHAPTER 11

Open to the Public

*He that is greedy of gain
troubleth his own house.*
Proverbs 15 xxvii

They rattled at the bars of the cage and gibbered at him as he sat
in his deck-chair smoking a small cigar and sipping from the beaker
that his attendant had brought him. He looked at them with cool
contempt. Although they were closely related to him they were,
nevertheless, a different species: so physically degenerate that many
of them would die if released into the bush and jungle which
encroached upon the site of the zoo in which he was a guest. He
finished his drink, flicked away his cigar and strolled over towards
the front of the cage. The mocking howls and obscene gestures
redoubled at his approach. He scrutinised the rabble for a minute
then, as if to express his resulting opinion, he peed upon them
through the bars of his cage. Turning his back upon the shouts of
indignation and fury he made a swing and a spring on to a shelf
which had been built into a corner, settled down comfortably and
went to sleep.

He was a Coriolanus of a gorilla. I remembered him and tried
to emulate his example of indifference to an audience as we lunched
in the vast dining-room of Matthew's house. A large crowd of
trippers stood outside, gawping through the windows at us in
fascinated curiosity. Some, in order to see us more clearly, shaded
their eyes against the reflection of the glass and pressed their faces

. . . . gawping through the windows . . .

hard against the panes; one tapped hesitantly, as of a person wishing to attract the attention of a nest of snakes in the reptile house.

"Can I get down and stare back?" asked Candy.

"Certainly not, it's rude," said her mother. "Ignore them and they'll get bored and go away."

"No they won't," said our host. "Some of them are far more interested in the people who live in stately homes than in the houses themselves, or the furniture and works of art. I spend my life like a goldfish in a bowl. I rather like it," he concluded smugly.

After lunch we strolled round his park and gardens. Groups of people sat on the grass, surrounded by the debris of their picnics.

"Each of those plastic mugs that you see scattered about has come from one of my drink-dispensing machines and has given me four pence profit," Matthew said. "Look at those people rowing on the moat – it costs almost nothing to look after the boats and I charge fifty pence for twenty minutes. That queue over there is to see our collection of model steam engines which my father built between his stays in the looney bin, fifteen pence a head. Those longer queues are for the lavatories, I charge for their use, but haven't found a way of making a profit from them – yet. Over there, in that little booth, is where we sell mementos and souvenirs: mugs and ashtrays with transfer pictures of the house on them, place-mats and trays with reproductions of the Elizabethan map of the village and estate, and pottery made by old Brigadier Doxon who lives in the lodge.

"There's the 'Kiddies' Korner and Kreche'. Basically that's the old tennis court with a sandpit at one end and a few cuddly rabbits, squirrels and other vermin. Parents can dump their brats in it for a bit of peace. Ms O'Tool, a part-time schoolmistress, collects the money – fifty pence a child – and keeps an eye on them to see that they don't climb the fencing or get bitten by the animals.

"Best of all are the Dungeons. Luckily my Great-Great-Great-Grandfather shut up my Great-Great-Great-Grandmother in the cellars for a few years and it's rumoured that he tortured her, so I've hung up some chains and manacles on the walls and got Mr Dewbit to forge some thumbscrews and pincers and put them in a glass-fronted case. We have a good collection of man-traps which we've used against poachers over the last three hundred years; there is part of a pole-trap made for catching hawks by their legs – I've put it in a case on its own and most people think that it's a chastity belt; there is Great-Aunt Tourmaline's cupboardful of whips; an Egyptian mummy – a bit mildewed; Cousin Arabella's collection of circumcision knives; some shrunken heads which Papa brought back from Borneo – one looks European so I put a strip of white cardboard round its neck and it now looks a bit like Canon Holt; the skeleton of a woman we found down the well in the courtyard. Our prize exhibit is Uncle Percy's silken rope and noose.

"I charge one pound for admittance.

"Now, you haven't got a stately home, but you've written a book about your garden and say that people come and look at it – you could make some money out of that. Once you've got them in your clutches you could attract them with all sorts of tantalising things, particularly the women: your friend, Firecrest, is always quoting Ovid who said, over two thousand years ago, 'a woman is always buying something.'"

Dominie and I discussed Matthew's ideas as we drove home. We did not like them: it seemed inhospitable to ask money from people – most of whom were very pleasant – who came to see the garden, and we did not want to attract additional crowds of strangers and thus ruin our privacy. Nevertheless, I could see some logic to the basic theme, for the garden was becoming scruffy because of our unexpected guests and it seemed reasonable to get them to pay towards the costs of repairing this. The main cause was wear and tear, especially Gnat Walk and parts of the lawns which were being eroded by the tramping of feet. Amazingly, although we told callers that we thought of them as our guests, some repaid this hospitality with vandalism: pulling out plants, snapping off twigs and leaving litter – even chucking bottles and cans into the ponds. Also I was becoming abashed about the state of the garden. It has never been very tidy, I am merely a weekend gardener and Hart, who is now eighty, only works for two days a week, so I have often overheard scornful mutters of amazement from people seeing our luxuriant growths of shepherd's purse, devil's guts and ground elder. If all these visitors were asked to pay their basic costs, we could spend their money as wages on young Junkett, the milkman's son, who would do an extra day's weeding, and on grass seed to recover the bald patches scalped by sandal, shoe and boot.

A long period of paying death duties had made Matthew cynical and grasping, we had no wish to emulate his attitude, but we saw no harm in the idea that if we had a collection of potential customers there were extra offers which we could put before them which could be both pleasing to them and profitable to us. As the people would be visiting us in order to see the garden, it was apparent that the items which would be interesting to them would be concerned with gardening, but there could also be a chance to start up my special fixation, a scheme I had been brooding about for several years: the Farm Shop.

Dominie and I undertook some market research in the local garden centres. A few were specialists, most concentrating on roses, which grow particularly well in our area, or on trees, for which there is always a demand from farmer, landlord and local council; others were even more specialised and dealt only with a single aspect, such as rare plants, or lilies, or dry gardens, or silver foliage. However, most garden centres we saw had a much broader scope and sold almost everything to do with horticulture, not only plants but also implements, chemicals, rocks and flagstones, conservatories, swimming pools, bird tables, books, seeds and bulbs, jam, pet-foods and rides at ten pence a go on mechanical Triffids.

When I was about thirteen my parents had a London flat near Harrods, the Knightsbridge shop, and I used to like to visit the pet department which not only was stocked with mundane pets such as puppies and kittens, but also contained much more pleasurable creatures such as adders, grinning little crocodiles and white rats with eyes like blood-crazed currants. By a fearsome feat of bad planning the pet section had been surrounded by another department which was labelled CORSETRY AND LADIES' UNDERWEAR. Small boys were obliged to speed through it, cheeks burning and eyes lowered modestly to their twinkling, prep-school issue shoes.

"Everybody is looking at me and thinking that I am interested in the stays."

In fact, no one thought anything of the sort.

And so they were wrong: secretly, small boys were fascinated by those rum, complicated and rather rude thingeys which women wore under their frocks.

There are no such psychological barriers in the Albert Garside Garden Centre. Customers are cajoled up the drive which is edged by an immaculate avenue of shrubby borders; they are soothed into a gravelled car-park which is in an artificial glade. The artistically arranged trees round about it are separated by small areas paved with concrete flags, each furnished with a "rustic" bench and a large yellow litter-bin and indicated by the words 'Picnic Bower and Rest Nooke' engraved in Gothic script on deckle-edged slabs of elm. Near the main entrance is a fenced-off impoundment containing a climbing frame and a row of plastic rocking horses. From the invitingly open portals of the adjacent building can be heard, trilling, the song of caged canaries and can be smelt, wafting, a pleasant scent which is a subtle mixture of honey, roses and potting compost.

Albert Garside snuggled his seventeen-stone bulk into the comfortable chair by his desk and explained the psychological basis of the layout. His candid lack of secrecy was because he was an old MI6 associate of my father who, during the war, always chose Albert when there was any need for a ruthless and efficient explosives saboteur to be sent into occupied Europe. In those days

Albert Garside was known as Stanislaus Gryzinski and weighed only ten and a half stone; it is amazing what age can do to a person.

"Well, lad," he replied to my questioning, "happens it comes this way, betimes," and he drew thoughtfully at his old briar pipe. "First tha separates thy customers from their kiddies so that there's no irritating distraction from job in hand (buying the articles laid out for sale). Each little tot is more destructive to a flowering plant than a whole plague of locusts – or a formation of Stukas. People come here to buy plants, so that is what they are led to at its beginning: first, house plants in the Main Hall then, once they step outside they come face to face with a mass of potted favourites, primulas, begonias and such like; then the bargain of the week, a rose or hedging plant for example; finally, the general sales area divided up into fruit, trees, shrubs, climbers, herbaceous plants and the rest. Now, unless you've got a hell of a lot of money, start your business small and develop by degrees. Merge your plant sales with the farm shop you are thinking about, and see what sells and what doesn't, and find out where your customers come from. You have already started, with the Christmas trees that Tony Crisp sells every year. Buy in some popular potted flowers, cyclamen and African violets can always be re-sold at a reasonable profit, and plant something which grows easily on your soil: roses, clematis and water plants, for example."

We decided to take much of his advice, though this did not include growing roses or clematis because there are already some very good local nurseries dealing with these. I investigated a variety of other options and finally chose willows and poplars. These species of tree are related and thus have many similarities: they usually like damp soil, they often strike easily from cuttings, they can seed rapidly in moist ground, they grow fast; they have a wide range of conformations including creeping, weeping, fastigiate, prostrate, round-headed, flat-topped and pointed; many have brightly coloured bark, usually on the young shoots, others have attractive catkins. Hillier's *Manual of Trees & Shrubs* gives about four pages on poplars and nine on willows; Bean mentions about seventy varieties of the former and two hundred and seventy of the latter. As well as being ornamental, some can be sold in bulk to other specialists: poplars to landowners who will grow them in plantations and eventually sell them for matchwood or for shaving into strips which are then woven into punnets; osiers for wicker-workers, and Lombardy poplars to builders and councils for screening.

We decided to start up the nursery in some disused water meadows called Cambridge Meadows. I suppose it is so called because Cambridgeshire, to our locals in the old days, was a flat area of boggy ground. It was inhabited by "Cambridgeshire Camels", so called because they had to wade long-legged through their fens and swamps on stilts. The other fenlanders, the men from Lincolnshire, were called "yellow-bellies", not a slur on their courage: they had been turned yellow by the ague which bred in their bogs and dykes. The rest of the world was lumped together in one dismissive phrase – "the Shires" – which excluded, of course, our close neighbours: those from over the Stour were generally considered to be "one noggin to the bushel" and were called Suffolk Simples.

I have surveyed the field names of the estate. Many names have been erased since the arrival of the combine harvester, a machine which prefers a field of thirty acres or more. When I was a boy it was rare to walk through a field of over eight acres. There used to be a common saying throughout England: "Essex stiles, Kentish miles and Norfolk wiles, many men beguiles", referring to the fact that Essex had a mass of tiny fields, each joined to its neighbour with a wooden stile in a hedge. Many of our hedges have now been grubbed up by the tenant farmers, but these hedges are relatively recent, planted during the plethora of enclosures in the seventeenth and eighteenth centuries. Thus the removal of hedges has restored the appearance of the countryside to that of the Tudor period, when there were a few large, irregular enclosures and commons rather than a mass of small, usually straight-sided fields. But a change back to the past is not necessarily a good thing, and in this case the loss of wild flora and fauna has been immense. I try to compensate for this destruction by planting spinneys and copses in field corners or around dew ponds, but a clump of trees is a poor substitute for a hedge because it cannot act as a pathway for all the small creatures who need to travel, nor is there such a wide variety of different habitats. A hedge has a verge, a ditch, a thicket, an undergrowth and a high canopy, but a spinney usually has only the last two. Millicent has told this to me often, but such is the reproving and sanctimonious air with which she speaks I often feel like replying that I shall grub up every bush and replace it with a petrol station or casino.

We have an estate map, a large, unwieldy sheet of linen-reinforced paper about six foot by nine. It is dated 1885, the year my Great-Grandfather bought the land for his eccentric daughter who wanted to be a farmer and who wore men's clothes. The map is greatly out-of-date, for it includes land my father had to sell because of Sir Stafford Cripps' capital levy after the war, and also it excludes woods and cottages which my family have planted or built in nooks and corners. We have a reproduction of an older map of the parish, dated 1777 and scaled at two inches to the mile. It is not helpful as far as fields are concerned for it does not mark them, but it is interesting in that it shows houses which have now gone, and roads which have almost disappeared. It is surprising to see that there were more roads in those days than there are now and what we see as green lanes or merely bridle paths were then busy with pack horses and waggons.

Last year we had a "Bygones" show in the parish church. The exhibits included smocks, wheelwright's equipment, butter churns, bean barrows, embroidery, sparrow nets, flails and a hundred other things which the parishioners had found in their attics, in their rafters or on their chimney-shelves. My contributions were an ox-yoke, a gleaner's rake, a miniature loom of a type used ninety years ago in our local weaving shed, a baulk of timber on a chain which had been the hobble for a cart horse and some photographs of the farm and estate taken before the First World War.

To me, the most interesting item was produced by the rector: the village Tithe Map. It is dated 1833 and shows every household and every field, together with their names. Like the children's game "Chinese Whispers", names have been transformed with time and use: Pelsons to Peldons, Great White House Field to Great White Horse Field, Bridge Wicks to Bridgetts, Boosins Green to Booseys Green (and now some people are calling it Boozers' Green). In other cases the names have vanished either, because several small fields have been amalgamated into a large one, or for some other reason: Ivy Croft has changed into Spitfire Field because of the aeroplane which crash-landed there during the war; I changed Fen Field and the Old Hop Ground into Coppin's Wood when I planted trees there and wanted a memento of Big

Sam's family who had farmed there; Peldons Meadow changed into the Shooting Ground after Monk built a clay pigeon tower in it; Dark Meadows has changed to Below Nancy's, Mill Field to By Jack's and Westwood Pasture to the Young Stallions.

Some of the field names are inexplicable: why Blue Bottles, Coat Field, Second Folly and Bearings Field? Some names refer to past activities of which there is now no sign, the evidence lives in the names only: Cash Bridge Field – presumably a toll bridge on the brook at the bottom of the field – Stony Moat, the Quakers' Burial Ground and Blanket Field (the rent from this was spent on blankets for the parish poor). Some of the most useful names indicated the purposes or the opinions of the previous users: Goslings Pasture, Bullocks Valley, Osier Ground, Teasels, White Orchard, Sour Ley, Thistley Field, Too Good and 1000 Acres (the last two names being sarcastic – we have never harvested a good crop from Too Good's leached-out soil and 1000 Acres is a couple of chains long and one chain wide).

The field name Cambridgeshire Meadow correctly suggested that the area, like its namesake, would be suitable for the growing of poplars and willows. The land is rich and although not water-logged has a good flow of subterranean water. A brook runs along one side, suitable for the irrigation which will be needed during the dry season – and a local nurseryman told me that irrigation is very necessary in our area of low rainfall: he has ten acres of young trees ranging in age from year-old seedlings to four-year-old "whips" and in one dry summer he needed six million gallons of water to keep them alive.

One small area of the field is boggy, and Tony Crisp and I went to inspect it to see if it needed drainage. The swamp surrounded a small pond which my father had dug out thirty years before in order to keep trout. Unfortunately floods washed away the retain-ing gratings and the fish escaped into the brook. As neither of his sons showed much enthusiasm for fishing my father abandoned the pool to the encroaching vegetation. The area was now a mass of horse-tails, overtopped with willow and alder. The pool had vanished to be replaced by a large bright green glade of gummy ooze and half-submerged branches. As Tony and I clambered and waded through it, the squidgy ground and rotten vegetation emitted a cacophony of sucking, gurglings, squelching, gobblings and snappings, just like my youngest brother-in-law eating breakfast. A wisp of snipe fleeted off from a small glade. I noticed several clumps of interesting sedges. The sloughed-off skin of a grass snake lay at the foot of a guelder rose and in a thicket of blackthorn I spotted the remnants of a bottle tit's nest. I decided that, as there was plenty of space in the eight acres of the meadow which remained, I would allow that half acre to stay as a refuge for wildlife.

I thought that I would start our nursery with a choice of the most popular trees from our selected species: weeping willows, Lombardy poplars and the bushy willows which have interestingly coloured twigs or pretty foliage or catkins, such as the scarlet willow, the violet willow, the hoary (or rosemary-leafed) willow, Wehrhahnii, which has catkins like rabbits' scuts and Melanostachys, whose catkins are almost black.

The trade dealers in cricket-bat willows and osier stumps were also contacted, their needs analysed, the potential competition assessed, the marketing methods researched, and, finally, the saplings were planted: an operation which took two years to complete. The young stock was bought from other nurserymen, for it seems that much of the tree-selling trade has developed into two processes, firstly the production of the stock from seeds and cuttings, secondly, the nurturing of this stock into young trees, saplings, whips or shrubs.

We decided to sell these from a sales area by the main road. This would be convenient for any regular customers but, of even more importance, it would attract the "impulse buyers"; those passersby who suddenly decide to have a change from the tedious chore of driving their family to the seaside or their sales samples to the coldly critical scrutiny of their customers.

Having prepared the basis of the nursery, we turned our attention to the farm shop. Much of our information came from "Chipper" Matthews. He is a neat, spry man in his early seventies. As a youth, he had left his family farmstead for the stables of Newmarket and still looks like a successful jockey, invariably wearing whipcord breeches about his short, bowed legs and with a cravat flowing between the lapels of his brass-buttoned, baize waistcoat. He is usually accompanied by his trio of vast sons, amiable and scruffy, who loom above him like three kindly bears who have adopted a spider monkey. The family had toiled hard for many years on their eighty acres somewhere in the triangle between Little Maplestead,

Belchamp St Paul and Blackmore End. I have seen them in a twenty-acre field planting potatoes by hand: the boys lugging great sacks of seed potatoes, Chipper dibbling neat holes in rows and Mrs Matthews, always coughing, bent double as she dropped the potatoes down them and nudged the holes shut with the side of her foot. She finally died, of overwork we supposed, for in a typical way the men, although full of affection and kindliness, would no more dream of helping with the cooking when they all tottered home exhausted in the evening than they would have thought of making the beds or cooking breakfast before they set off to work next morning. However, old Chipper always used to open the door and let her through first, even if the last time he did it was to let her tired, dead body out, feet first, through their front gate. It was sadly ironic that a year after her death the family discovered an easier way to make a living.

The lane that meandered along the boundary of their land was suddenly changed into a main road as a result of a diversion. Thus throughout the year lorries thunder by from the ports of Harwich and Felixstowe to the business centres of the Midlands and West London, whilst throughout the summer a steady stream of tripper traffic, bound for Clacton or Southend, buzzes agitatedly past their farmyard gate. After a week of cursing the noise, the fumes and the prying eyes, Chipper, on an impulse, did something more constructive and put out a few sacks of potatoes by his gate together with a noticeboard which said:

KinG EDWarDS
STRATE From our Feilds
FARM PRICES!

He sold out in the first morning.

One drizzly afternoon I went to see Chipper to ask his advice about farm shops. He is a hard-headed man and will not disclose secrets that would be to his loss, but I live away from his main road and out of his "catchment" area; also he is a friend of Monk, who came with me. Hart came, too, as the gardening expert.

The wooden shack by their farm entrance was packed. Herbert, the youngest son, was weighing out a sack of maize for a bent little old couple with Birmingham accents. "Not a brace of teeth between them, they'll not scrape many corns off those cobs," hissed Monk at me. John, the eldest son, was loading a Mini with two sacks of potatoes and a bunch of chrysanthemums and Garth, the middle son, was painstakingly calculating and re-calculating the cost of ten dozen eggs which had been bought by a group of firmly argumentative nuns. A cluster of waiting customers fidgeted behind the trestle table which served as a counter. Their cars were tidily arrayed in rows on the concreted yard which blighted the appearance of the timbered farmhouse.

Mr Matthews sat on an upturned crate, smoking a Silk Cut held delicately between finger and thumb. His boots shone, and a tie pin twinkled in the silken folds of his cravat.

"Afternoon, Chipper," said Monk. "You're looking very flash, you just going out to get yourself a woman?"

"No, no, mate," said the old horseman, scandalised, "I hasn't had me tea yet."

We set ourselves around the scrubbed table in his kitchen. It was efficiently presided over by John's wife, who laid out little plates of goodies and poured us cups of tea.

"Cor, blast me, gal," Hart said to her after taking a great bite out of a yellow slab covered with pink icing and besprinkled with little silver balls, "I can see why this here cake is called a 'sponge', it's been and sucked all the juices out of me head!"

Chipper, ignoring this critical statement, proceeded to talk shop.

"Eggs and potatoes, that's what you want. The Min-of-Ag-and-Fish say that about two-thirds of all produce sold from farm shops is eggs. 'Free range', I call them; brown sells best, except to the Yanks from the airydrome, they're reverse to us and like their eggs white and their chicken meat yellow. We grow our potatoes, maize and broad beans. I tried strawberries and a few other fruits but couldn't compete with young Todmore over the valley: he's got a better touch with those than us, always fossicking over his plants, he is, so we buy them from him and resell. Bunches of flowers by the gate always attract customers but don't bring in that much money. Sally here keeps a few bee-hives, so we sell honey and have started at homemade jam. There's no end to it," and he rubbed his hands together and cackled.

He may be correct. But I am away at work during most of the day, Dominie is busy with ponies and children, and the others have their own jobs to do. We have started in a small way with our farm shop, but it rankles that the sign which attracts most customers, and which results in the best profits, simply says:

PONY MANURE FOR SALE

CHAPTER 12

The Outdoor Life

The chariots shall rage in the streets,
they shall justle one against another
in the broad ways.

Nahum 2 iv

I started my business career as a floor sweeper in a weaving shed. There were three lavatories in it. Their doors were variously inscribed: 'STAFF', 'Gentlemen' and 'L★A★D★I★E★S'. I knew that I did not fit into the latter category, in spite of receiving numerous letters insultingly addressed "Dear Sir or Madam", but I am still unsure which of the other two doors I should have used. I used 'STAFF' as it had proper loo paper, instead of ripped up squares of newspaper, and the graffiti rhymed more amusingly.

There is a similar indecision beween the recipients of two magazines: that of the Country Gentlemen's Association and of the Country Landowners' Association, but in this case I know that I am not a gentleman as I receive the latter and am thus able to read articles on such obscure subjects as "Turbot farming in the Outer Hebrides", "The restoration of medieval venison larders" and "Slag heaps into Ski slopes". One of the articles which I found particularly interesting concerned the enormous amount of money one could make out of caravan sites and the five million campers.

I was amazed when I read it. I had presumed that a caravanner is a romantic soul who wishes to meander through highways and byways to some secluded spot, there, at twilight, to pitch his tent, assemble and ignite a heap of faggots gleaned from a nearby grove, brew his rabbit and groundsel stew and then, to the drowsy lullabies of nightingales and crickets, drift off to sleep amidst the scents of honeysuckle and new-mown hay as the trees that surround his roost dapple the ground with their moon-made shadows.

Not a bit of it. He drives off to a licensed caravan site. This is often an officially approved eyesore which, being situated in an attractive part of the country – a dale, vale, peak or lake – renders that spot hideous with serried rows of cream-coloured caravans and orange tents, the only attractive views being those to be seen from the site itself. Having thus gone to the country in company with several hundred other caravans, each of which contains, on average, 2 adults, 1.7 children, 0.68 dogs and 3 daily attacks of the collywobbles, the caravanner then expects entertainment and amenities. He expects lavatories, hot water and electricity; he may even expect to shop in the communal shop, to play bingo or whist in the community hall and, to the recorded bawlings of the top twenty hits, to dance the night away. There may be play areas for his children and sandpits for his dogs. If he is very stoical he will allow himself to be assailed by the roar of engines and the stink of petrol fumes as his daughter water-skis and his son motorcycle-scrambles in areas set out nearby.

I thought this article in the magazine to be exaggerated, so one evening I went for advice to Bradawl, who is a keen caravanner.

He was sitting in his kitchen reading a book on the carpentry of medieval house construction. His boots were off and his wig snugly draped on his teapot, keeping both warm.

"That's quite right," he said, after I had shown him the article. "The sort of caravanning that you think people like is left for a few lunatics like that chap Rufus; come, I'll show you mine."

He popped his comfily warm wig on top of his head, stepped into his boots and led me out to the back of his garden. There, at the end, was a colossal hutch on wheels. Inside, the only similarity it had to Rufus' waggon was the orderly neatness and the plenitude of cupboards, but many of these contained the most modern electrical or gas-operated gadgets: a boiler, toaster, oven, frying pan, kettle, wireless, television and thermostatically controlled blankets. The most noticeable difference was the feeling of light and airy fragility: most things in the gypsy caravan were constructed from heavy wood, brass and leather, and were shrouded in heavy gloom; in Bradawl's conveyance the pale cream and green surfaces of the enamelled metal and plastic reflected the light coming through the windows which comprised over half the wall space.

"You could call this more of a mobile house than a caravan," said Bradawl. "The point of having one of these is to go to a nice place and live there as comfortably and as conveniently as possible. We almost always go to the same place at the same time: a site by the sea in Pembrokeshire, during the first fortnight in July; we know that many of the friends that we have made will be there, too, and it's nice to see familiar faces again."

Next day I went to see Rufus. He was lounging back on the steps of his caravan, watching Gloria through half-closed eyes as she clipped his toe-nails. Karen was scything some rough grass along a hedgerow in the distance and Millicent was putting some clothes in a cauldron which hung over the fire. Hippocampus munched, Frodo tweeted and The August-Personage-in-Jade glowered.

"During the three years that you've been on the road, how many people have you met who were deliberately holidaying 'gypsy style'?"

"Hardly any, squire," he said. When bored, he liked to be annoying, and he had discovered it irked me to be called "squire" almost as much as it irked Monk to be called the "Hedge Hopper" or Hart "Walter Gabriel".

"There's a little firm I know which hires out proper caravans, but most people keep away from it after they have been shown the complications of harnessing and driving a horse. And if they pitch camp away from their fellow humans, they get panic-struck during their first night by owls hooting and twigs cracking and rabbits squealing."

I did not entirely believe all this advice. I was convinced that there would be at least a few people who would like a proper country holiday in rural surroundings: an attractive, secluded site; perhaps the opportunity to gather their own food, a spot of fishing, a bit of ferreting, the gleaning of herbs and berries; and of course, the ponies. They could go for a ride in the pony trap, or they could trek; I had seen many fly-posters near my London office urging people to go pony trekking in Wales or the Peak District.

The first consideration was the site. It had to be amongst trees, near running water, have attractive views and, although being reasonably far from the road, yet be accessible to cumbersome caravans towed by small cars. I eventually whittled the number of possible sites to three.

The first was the disused railway line.

Once, the train used to tell me when it was going to rain. It started off from Haverhill and pottered down the valley towards the sea. It was small and square and had a tall funnel which puffed clouds of smoke and spat geysers of red-hot cinders which often set the embankments alight during summer, and it pulled three carriages and a weather-boarded guard's van. It seemed that there were always three passengers, no more, and when we children waved at the train chugging past they would wave back very slowly as if in a dream. The driver had a grey spade-beard and he, too, would wave back whilst his mate crouched intently over the controls. There was a shunting yard in the station of Halstead, about three miles up-stream, which was always a bustle of activity, as they shuffled and buffeted waggons from one siding to another, changed round flat-cars of bricks and truck loads of moos and bleats, or container loads of grain with pallets holding warps for our local weaving shed and, always, cargo – to keep the track working – coal, railway sleepers and ballast. This work went on all day and late into the evening. When I lay in bed, if the weather was to be fine next day, all I could hear was the whisper of the wind in the trees outside, but if it were to rain I would hear the muffled panting, puffing, bumping and clanks as the Colne Valley trains went about their business.

The railway line was killed; the bridges pulled down, the line ripped up and the men sacked in an act of economic and social vandalism. My father had to buy about a mile of the old trackway as he owned the land at either side. Some of it he had levelled into the adjoining fields, but this was not possible with a four hundred yard length which was elevated above the surrounding land. This elevation gave this piece of land a pleasant view over water meadows or through cricket-bat willow plantations to the river. The track still had a firm and well-drained surface of hogging and clinkers. Trees had grown and thickets had sprouted. Many wild flowers had taken over, including two of my favourites, the grass vetchling, with its scarlet pea-like flower, and the hairy St John's wort, with its sunburst of stamens. The only intrusion into the

peaceful life of the rabbits or nesting partridges was the occasional
visit of Monk, or the rarer and more stealthy visits of Pinkhorn,
the poacher, with his lurcher, or of Hot-Hands Honeyball, the
village Romeo, with his latest "little bit of crackling". The combined width of the track and its verges averages a chain (22 yards
or the length of a cricket pitch) so there would be room to park
caravans. The only disadvantage was that the line of caravans
would be visible from parts of the village and, as I want to stay
on good terms with my neighbours, I thought it unwise to proceed.

The second option was Hungercroft Farm. The farmhouse had
burned down sixty years ago and was never rebuilt, but a huddle
of out-buildings still exist: a pair of open-fronted cart lodges, a
thatched hovel, stables fronting a livestock yard and a vast old
barn. All these centre upon a horse pond, its shallow stretch of
stagnant water edged with rank patches of nettles and brambles or
overcast with alders and a crack willow, whose splintered bole can
just be seen amongst the shattered and contorted remnants of its
fallen branches. The site overlooks a valley created by a small
brook.

Unfortunately Monk was most averse to the inhabitation of the
site, as three of his best pheasant-holding spinneys are nearby and
caravans, he reckoned, contained infestations of children and dogs
which would be a blight to his birds. Dominie was equally unen-
thusiastic, for some of her ponies inhabit the out-buildings whilst
the undulating and well-drained slopes which lead down to the
brook are used by her for "herding", where she lets out a selected
stallion with his harem of mares.

So, although Hungercroft Farm was a good potential site for
caravanners, it was a better site for ponies and I had therefore to
opt for my third possibility, a ride in Hadrian's Wood.

I have always been fond of King John and disliked his brother,
King Richard, mainly because everyone else thinks the opposite,
but there is also a more logical reason for my prejudice, like the
small child who wrote: "Everybody loves Baby Jesus even my
uncle and both my bruthers but I don't, I luv the three wizmen
best becus they broat presence." John was popular in our area for
he brought much prosperity to it and he defended the people
against the greedy tyranny of the local barons and churchmen
until, finally, they forced him to grant them despotic powers by
agreeing to the Magna Carta. Poor fidgety and harassed John was

probably the most restless of all our kings, travelling ceaselessly over his realm, often up to thirty miles a day. Thus no other monarch was as personally acquainted as was he with the villages and towns, lanes and rivers, moors and marshlands and other little-known by-ways of the Kingdom. During these forays he often stayed in Colchester Castle; he also had a palace at Writtle, all that remains of which is a dried-out moat and a fish pond. One of his greatest pleasures when staying in these places was to hunt the boar in a local forest, which over the years has been eroded into a fragmentation of smaller woods: one of these is Hadrian's Wood. This eighty-acre expanse is approximately the shape of a kidney – or a broad bean, if you are a vegetarian like Millicent. One half is bounded by the remains of a ditch and hedge bank, so old that they are mere undulations in the ground. When digging a ditch one throws the soil on to one's own land, not the neighbour's, thus a man who owns a hedge usually owns the ditch the other side of it, because the hedge is planted on the bank. Monk says the reverse happens in a deer park, for if the newly planted hedge is accessible to the deer it will be eaten. Much of the bank and hedge in Hadrian's Wood is on the outer side so we presume it was once a deer park. Because of its great age, the wood is full of well established wild plants such as wood anemone, dog's mercury, enchanter's nightshade, ramsons, honeysuckle and broad buckler fern in the darker places, foxglove, bugle, raspberry and teasel in the rides and glades, toothwort and beefsteak fungus on the rotting timber and, in spring, a shimmering ocean of bluebells. For many years the wood had been coppiced. Although some of the better indigenous trees had been left as standards, they were mainly oaks, small-leafed lime or gean. Most of the area had been planted with the traditional coppicing blend of chestnut-with-hazel. These, harvested on a regular basis, supplied a steady income; the rot-resistant and cleavable chestnut being sold for fence posts, hop poles, gates and ladder rungs; the sturdy and pliable hazel for wattling, hurdles, brotches (hair-pin shaped pegs used by thatchers), baskets, barrel hoops for the "slack casks" used by grocers, fish traps, pea sticks, ships' fenders, fascines for river banks, clothes pegs and water-divining crutches.

Bradawl can water divine, and was propounding on the subject in the kitchen one day.

Hart took another biscuit from a tin, washed it down with a noisy gulp of tea and having prepared himself for debate said, "I don't hold with all them cranky notions; I reckon all that there twitchings and strainings that I've seen you do is because you know there's water there already."

Bradawl bridled. "You come along with me," he said crossly. "There's an underground stream runs through this garden, I'll tell Tony here where it is, and it might be that you can find it."

We all traipsed out of the kitchen and re-assembled at the end of the ride which bisects the Pinetum. Bradawl cut out a V-shaped hazel crutch from the road hedge nearby and told Hart how to hold it as he walked back towards the house. Grumbling with coyness at the massed attention being paid to him, Hart stumped off, his clenched fists level with his eyes as he gripped the two arms of the twig so that the point of the V was directed to his destination, the front door. He passed solemnly and cynically below the firs and pines, between the floriferous and weediferous lushness of the herbaceous borders and then, after about two hundred yards, he entered the Rose Garden. There were forty yards to go before he reached the house and he opened his mouth to scoff. Instead, his jaw dropped even further, for the point of the twig had jerked towards the ground. His eyes popped, the wiry muscles on his arm tightened like ropes as he tried to force the point up again.

"Walk on!" shouted Bradawl, and Hart cautiously stepped forward; with each stride the twig, shaking and vibrating under the strain of his biceps, twitched further towards the ground and his expression intensified its combination of amazement, awe and reluctant pride.

"Cor, damn my eyes, well I'm blessed," he kept on breathing. Finally the crutch was pointing directly between his feet. "That's where I was told the water is, level with this white rose," said Tony. Hart walked on and the point of the twig rose again. He dropped it and looked at the palms of his hands, there were scuff marks and weals and the ball of his right thumb showed blood. We all then tried to do it, but no one else had the "touch".

Back to Hadrian's Wood. Once we had stopped coppicing, the uncut butts grew tall suckers which eventually turned into trees and the overhead canopy began to kill some of the more interesting plants with its heavy shade. Monk complained that the rides were becoming so narrow that the guns had no time to see the birds that he sent over them. I therefore widened the three main drives to the breadth of about three and a half chains; they were about ten chains long, thus each ride averages about three and a half acres. The result is most attractive: green swarth has replaced the brambles and dewberry which had become the dominant and smothering growth in the heavy shade, the towering lines of trees which edge the rides give them an air of seclusion and sanctity, and fallow deer can often be seen wandering amongst the spires of foxglove and patches of bluebell.

Below the wood, and parallel to its length, a brook runs, so clear and fresh that it holds trout and crayfish.

The only problem for any caravanners would be the access, for the nearest lane to the wood is two fields away and the only approach is along an old green road, which had become deeply rutted by the wheels of farm vehicles and by Monk's Land-Rover.

I made a plan of action, the details of which caused the faces of Dominie and Monk to turn grim with foreboding, Dominie because she thought that the scheme would not succeed, Monk because of his pheasants.

"We will offer them an idyllic site in secluded and restful surroundings; we can have extras, which they will pay for: fishing in the brook and riding and driving."

It took three months to prepare the site. Most of the work was undertaken by Tony Crisp, Bradawl or my children, when there was nothing more urgent. The priority was the green road, it had to have its ruts filled in and its surface made hard lest its condition be made even cruder by our vehicles. This was when the old railway track became useful once more: after we had bought it we found that the upper two feet of its surface was a constantly useful quarry of material for driveways and yards. We rented a bulldozer and Tony drove it along the green lane, with its blade angled sideways. He then drove it back with its blade angled in the opposite direction so that, each way, the blade had pushed the uneven top surface into the adjacent meadows. After four hours' more work this surplus mush had been spread evenly over the fields. The bulldozer then clanked slowly off, like an arthritic tortoise, to the railway track and scraped up some of the hard surface into heaps; these Tony loaded on to a trailer and dumped and spread on to the green road. We also hired a quaint little machine which rapidly hopped up and down as it advanced, like a stunted flamenco dancer, it was called a Vibrating Roller and it compacted the surface into road-like hardness.

During the two months that this was taking place, the boys and I were carving camping sites along the edge of the ride. I decided that they would all be on the same side, for if they were on both sides the campers would be able to see each other and would thus lose the feeling of seclusion and privacy. Each would be about thirty yards wide, which meant that there would be five sites per ride. We decided to deal with one ride only to start with, in case the notion proved to be a failure. George, Charlie and I cleared the sites. We situated them so no good trees need be felled, though some needed a few lower branches lopped; most of the work involved the clearing of undergrowth and brush. Some of the coppice stumps were poisoned to stop resprouting and then trimmed into flat-topped seats or tables. Pits were dug and then lined with bricks for hearths, a small heap of firewood was stacked invitingly beside each one. Some of the small poles that we felled were set aside for Bradawl; he arrived one day with a bag of nails, a hammer and a saw and within forty-eight hours he had made a suite of two chairs and a settle in "rustic" style for each site. We composed a leaflet which contained a short welcome and a long list of rules, the latter being mainly thought up by Monk, and Henrietta stencilled some copies of these in her secretarial college. Dominie's 500-gallon water-carrier was filled with fresh water and towed to a site at the top of the ride. An advertisement, ecstatically extolling the site and its lack of amenities was placed in a magazine for caravanners.

Nobody replied.

I was disconcerted by this overwhelming indifference. After some indignant brooding, I was forced to admit that much of the previous advice had been correct and that the average caravanner would not be attracted to the Spartan charms of Hadrian's Wood. My next advertisement was therefore put in a London evening paper and *The Times*.

There were four answers.

The first letter was written in sepia ink on green writing paper, sepia-coloured also were the engraved squirrels which nibbled acorns on the top right-hand corner and the harvest mouse which climbed a stalk of wheat up the left margin. The handwriting was elaborate, with curly crosses to the "Ts" and circles instead of dots over the "Is" and at the fullstops. The name of the house was Ferny Dingle, the writer was Angie Grospottle (Ms). The second letter was starkly simple in contrast: written on a small rectangle of lined paper in handwriting that was painstakingly neat but with spelling which was as bad as mine. The address was in Wapping and the writer, a Mr Henry Chapman, briefly informed me that he was interested in both the fishing and the absence of crowds and that Mrs Chapman would devote much of her time to her hobby of brass rubbing. The third letter, from a Knightsbridge mews, was written on very thick writing paper. The script was miniscule and appeared to have been written with a pin. It was almost completely illegible so, although the letter was extremely long, we could only fathom out that the writer was a poet and was looking for inspiration and seclusion. His signature looked like the death throes of a centipede, but fortunately his name was engraved flamboyantly above his address: Dashford Cawder, BA (Eng.) Cantab.

The last letter took two weeks to reach us as the writer had written "Sussex" instead of "Essex" on the envelope. His scribbled note told us that Mr and Mrs Edwin Scatterwell, together with their six children, would be arriving in time for tea on opening day.

Dai Plimsoles is a keen fisherman, so in exchange for some free angling in the brook, he agreed to take up the unallocated space with his horsebox which, like ours, has living quarters, and act as host: receiving guests if they arrived during my absence and keeping a protective eye on them.

Angie Grospottle was dressed almost entirely in crochet work: shawls, skirt, sash, bobble hat, she looked rather like those dolls some people put over their telephones or lavatory paper. A pair of short white socks and sandals added a touch of lamb to the general effect of mutton. Her companion, Miss Pilchards, was nondescript in a fussy collection of browns and greys which, with her beady little eyes and sharp nose, gave her the appearance of a moulting wren, an appearance accentuated when she peered out of the window of the caravan which seemed little bigger than a bird-box. On arrival, the two women ran excitedly about the leafy floor of the wood, peering at fern fronds, looking under logs,

turning over tufts of moss and tweeting at each other in ecstatic
pleasure.

The poet arrived next, in a Dormobile, a sort of van which had
been made into a caravan. I had expected the conventional poet
figure: burning eyes, consumptive cough, nicotine-stained fingers,
suede shoes and a large hat and cloak. I was therefore disappointed
to meet someone my age who was a caricature of my generation
twenty years ago: National Service haircut, tweed jacket with
leather buttons, a duffel coat and a likeable but puggy face with
freckles. Upon his arrival his camp-site sprouted an easel, side
tables, and a portable seat of canvas and aluminium which he sat
upon and proceeded to paint the view in a pleasant, rather Chinese
style with watercolours, the landscape being succinctly summarised with a few deft brush strokes to outline the edges of the ride,
the course of the brook and the crest of the valley ridge beyond; a
few streaks of undulations indicated tree-tops, branches, boles and
bushes. When Dai Plimsoles introduced us, Mr Cawder had just
completed his first picture and I said that I thought that he was a
poet, not a painter. Without any extra talk he led us into his
Dormobile. The walls were lined with his pictures; apparently to
emphasise the Chinese influence a squiggle of calligraphy unravelled
down one side of each painting. On closer inspection, however,
the squiggles proved to be short poems in his minute writing,
extolling the view depicted.

The Chapmans were short and comfortable and Cockney; they
arrived in a medium caravan pulled by a medium car, and after a
pause to brew a pot of tea, have a quick look at their environs,
and tell us that he had been a bus driver and she a clippie, and that
they had three children and nine grandchildren, they produced a
large amount of impedimenta to take to the brook, including two
deck-chairs, a bag holding some women's magazines together with
a bundle of knitting and half a dozen bottles of stout, a green
umbrella, cases of rods, a compartmented tin containing hooks,
lines and sinkers, and tins and tubes of assorted creams and lotions.
Dai Plimsoles and I helped them carry this baggage downhill to
the spot Mr Chapman had chosen during his reconnaissance. Mrs
Chapman plonked herself in her deck-chair, removed her cardigan
and, having applied anti-mosquito cream on to her chubby limbs,
she picked up a magazine, leant back in her chair and fell asleep.
Beside her, Mr Chapman fossicked and fiddled with his equipment

until he was finally able to flick his lure into the still waters under the roots of an alder on the opposite bank. He put his rod on a little aluminium stand, opened a bottle of stout, poured it as carefully into his glass as if it had been nitroglycerine and then settled himself into his chair with such a smile of blissful contentment on his cherubic face that I felt our efforts had all been worthwhile, if only to see someone so utterly content.

The Scatterwells arrived a day late. We had two telephone calls from them during the night, the first to say they had lost their way, the second to say that their car had temporarily broken down. I was there when they finally arrived: a huge and ramshackle caravan pulled by one of those nasty little German cars that look like ingrowing toenails; it was much too small for the job and its engine screamed with the effort of lugging its colossal appendage along the yielding surface of the ride. It contained a sweating driver and three children. Another foreign car followed containing a harassed looking woman with mousy tousles flopping over her eyes and three more children, one of whom shot rapidly out of the car when it stopped and was sick. The door of the first car opened and a brace of terriers sprang out, yapping, and disappeared at full pelt into the recesses of the wood, followed by some children screaming at them to come back. Two of the remaining children were told to unload, which they did by lugging out the contents of the cars and strewing them around the site. The final child, a repulsively sticky bundle which smelt like the corpse of a hippopotamus putrefying under the African sun, was extracted from the recesses of a car by its father. After some ineffectual and worried conversation with his wife he began reluctantly changing its nappy, his feelings on this task being made evident by spasmodic retchings.

His wife came up to me. "Where do we eat?" she grizzled, looking despairingly around her.

"Wherever you want," I replied expansively, indicating the whole site with a sweep of my arm. I pointed at the hearth and the heap of log wood.

"There's your kitchen."

She looked at them in hopeless bafflement and began to wring her hands.

"Ohdearohdearohdear," she whinged.

Her husband came up, mopping his brow. "What's wrong, Tattybuns?" he asked.

"We are meant to cook here, with these, on that."

"That's all right, we light the fire by rubbing two sticks together."

"Isn't it easier to use matches?"

"That's not the same; look, it's quite simple." He assembled a pile of paper and dried grass in the centre of the hearth and, kneeling beside it, began rubbing two twigs together frantically, like the back legs of an oversexed grasshopper. We all assembled in a respectful circle around him. He continued to chafe away. Steam began to rise, but from the top of his balding head rather than the twigs.

"I'm sure, dear, that you'll find matches more suitable," said his wife anxiously, watching his empurpling features.

"No, I bloody well won't," he snarled.

His brood began to lose interest and drift off, some to join the yapping and shouting which indicated the hunting activities of their dogs, some to pile into one of the cars and turn its wireless on at full pitch, others to explore the other camp-sites.

There was a bellow of rage, the sound of a slap and a screech. One of the children rushed back howling, followed by an infuriated poet.

"Who owns this meddling brat?" he shouted.

"He hit me!" it shruck.

"How dare you assail our Arnold!" they screamed.

Cawder shook his paint-brush under the noses of the agitated parents: "If any of your vile children fiddle with my easel again I'll shove this right up its arse."

"That's not a very nice thing to say; come, Edwin, we will ignore him."

I wandered down to the peace of the brook and sat down beside the Chapmans. Mrs Chapman opened the eye nearest me and said, "You've got a right little mob of terrors up there, luv, I reckon they'll give you a few sleepless nights before you see the last of them."

Mrs Chapman was correct: the children continued to fiddle with the painting equipment; one hooked itself when prying through Mr Chapman's tin case; they followed Angie Grospottle and Miss Pilchards so that the watching of birds and the photography of butterflies almost became an impossibility; they peered with awe-struck respect at the increasingly irritable poet from behind

trees and between bracken fronds; they uttered excited yells whenever anyone caught a fish and made snide comments whenever
either of the Chapmans opened another bottle of stout. Mrs Scatterwell was quite unable to cook on the hearth provided and so fed
her family entirely on crisps and biscuits and I had to spend half
my time picking up the resulting litter. The utterly useless father
had no control and spent most of his time under his cars, trying
to mend them, he said, but I thought it was to hide from his
increasingly repugnant and rebellious brood.

On their second day, Mr Scatterwell decided to go pony driving.

"Are you sure that you can drive a pony trap?" I asked uneasily.

"Quite sure," he replied, scowling fiercely at the ground.

"Oh, Edwin, are you certain that you're sure?" pleaded his
spouse.

"Absolutely. I think you are very rude to sound so disbelieving.
I used to drive my Auntie Dot's when I stayed on holiday with
her when I was a kid. I know all about it."

With the greatest reluctance, Dominie harnessed Bumble Bee to
the trap and drove him over the valley and up the green road to
the top of the ride. Mr Scatterwell and four of his children were
waiting, together with Dai Plimsoles who came up to us looking
fretful. He whispered, "That fellow has not a clue, I will hold the
little stallion by the bridle and lead them around and so it will be
that they shall come to no harm."

Mr Scatterwell climbed in and was obviously disconcerted that,
as it was a governess-cart, he had to sit sideways; Dai tactfully
reminded him how to hold the reins. His children scrambled in
after him: I was worried by their numbers but then thought that
the more, the safer, as their weight would slow down the pony.
Dai went up to Bumble Bee's head and held his bridle.

"Away," said Mr Scatterwell, pointing imperiously at him.

"Eh?" he asked.

"Away, my man. Go away. Stop hanging on to the horse."

The incensed Celt stepped aside.

"Giddy-yap!" shouted Mr Scatterwell and raising his whip high
in the air brought it down with a "thwack!' on the pony's fat
behind. For a second the pony froze, its eyes goggling with
disbelief and indignation. Then it bolted. It decided to go downhill
and it went like an express train. The children sent up a long wail
of terror. The driver howled "Woa, Woa, Woa" and sawed at the

. . . . its eyes goggling with disbelief . . .

reins. The only effect this had on the maddened beast was to change its course away from the centre of the ride towards the nearest camp-site. The poet was within, dabbling peacefully at a little water colour. He barely had time to blink twice before the doom-laden contraption had screamed past him and vanished into the woodland behind.

His experience was more fortunate than that of Angie Grospottle and Miss Pilchards.

The two women had discovered a glade, edged with great oaks above which they had noticed fast-flying specks, probably purple hairstreak butterflies. They set a honey-baited lure to attract the insects down so that they could be photographed. They built a hide of twigs and bracken to conceal their camera and themselves and then nestled inside, waiting breathlessly for the arrival of the fluttering friends.

The whole glade snoozed under the midday sun. Bees hummed, a pigeon murmured to its mate, a red admiral landed on the rim of the honey-laden saucer and prepared to sup. Ms Grospottle stretched out a stealthy finger towards the camera button. There was a thunderous "CRASH! WHUMP!", the bushes opposite the hide burst apart and through them charged a nightmare of starting eyeballs, bared teeth, flailing hooves, gesticulating arms, writhing bodies; wheels whizzed, metalwork flashed, the metal-tipped points of the two shafts pointed like javelins towards the appalled spinsters in their hide; the whole scene was partly hidden by a hail of leaves and clods of earth; from the centre of it all could be heard screams like a jamboree of banshees.

A wheel struck a tree stump and shattered, the cart overturned and threw its hysterical occupants to the ground. Bumble Bee fell under the weight of the cart. He tottered back to his feet and began sheepishly to graze. Miraculously, no one was hurt, just a few scratches and bruises.

Ms Grospottle emerged from her lair, trembling like a jelly. She gazed glassy-eyed at the splintered wreckage around her, at the snivelling children, and at Mr Scatterwell, who stood, swaying slightly, at the exact spot where there had once been a saucer of honey. Her eyes hardened as she looked at the abject figure, her lightly moustached upper lip lifted in a snarl of disdainful reproof. She spoke:

"You . . . you . . . you foolish . . . ." she paused for inspiration. It came: "You foolish *man*," she completed, and trembled back indignantly to her hide.

Scatterwell and family returned to their own home that afternoon and the other campers settled into the tranquillity that they had sought. When we finally counted all the costs and, far in excess of these, the amount of time spent in supervision and anxiety, I decided that the whole idea was not worth pursuing, unless we did it on a grand scale, but I prefer to leave the sleeping rides to the fallow deer and the foxgloves and the shade of King John. The Chapmans still come once a year, but I charge them nothing: the smiles of bliss on their faces as they settle down beside the brook, amidst the buttercups and alders, is payment enough.

As illogical and unprofitable a thought as that of keeping ponies.

CHAPTER 13

The Gourmets

. . . a feast of fat things, a feast of wines on the lees,
of fat things full of marrow, of wines on the lees well refined.

Isaiah 25 vi

Matthew has joined an organisation which finds paying guests to
live in private houses: holiday-makers, students and business-men
who want to stay a short while in the locality. He has up to twelve
guests at one time.

Sudbury, his butler, has grown fat on Arab tips.

One day, Matthew's rust-blotched Land-Rover rattled into our
yard. He peered worriedly at me from the driver's seat. "You
must help me," he said. "I've promised to organise a gourmet's
tour, and I don't even know what a gourmet is."

He waved a letter at me. "This is from that guest-finding
organisation I use. They say that they are going to run these
gourmet tours all over the country. Each tour will concentrate on
locally produced food and drink. It will be in private houses or
unconventional places only, no ordinary restaurants or hotels are
involved. Apparently I said I would help to run the one round
here. I don't remember saying so. I must have been drunk."

My heart hardened, whenever he gets into a muddle, Matthew
needs lots of time spent on him to sort things out.

He clambered out of the Land-Rover, lugging a large basket full
of asparagus after him. "From the kitchen garden," he said handing
it over, "and if you help me with this problem I'll see that you get

158

paid by the organisation for your advice." I began to think I could help him, after all.

He settled himself by my desk with a sigh while I read the letter. The average tour would last for twenty-four hours, it said. Guests, from six to a dozen, would have the following itinerary:

1. Arrive in the evening.
2. Dinner party.
3. Sleep.
4. Typical olde-Englishe breakfast.
5. A drive to somewhere interesting, there to look around.
6. Morning snack (tea and home-made sweets and biscuits).
7. Lunch.
8. Tea.
9. Buffet supper-cum-drinks party.
10. Train back to London.

". . . as you are aware," the letter continued, "a tour of inspection will be undertaken by our team of experts. They will judge the suitability of your arrangements. We are pleased to confirm that this tour will take place on Monday fortnight."

". . . and I've done nothing," Matthew moped. "For God's sake help me."

Monday was often a drab day for me when I was a child, for that was the day when the great old copper boiler was emptied of its delightful contents of pig-swill and filled with the mundane items of the weekly wash. The copper lived in a roofed alcove, just by the kitchen door. It was close enough for old Sophie to flip-flop out on her slippered feet and empty potato peelings, plate scrapings, stale bread and all the other edible refuse into the bubbling interior of the vat. Big Sam added to this mixture with shovel-loads of bran, and with butter-milk or whey from the products of Primrose, May, Buttercup and Betty Grable, the cows.

The resulting brew, warm and mealy, smelt delicious, and tasted even better, when licked off the end of a furtively dipped finger.

Three times a year the large copper bowl was lifted out of its platform and replaced by an enamelled one. In September we would fill this to the brim with fruit from the hedges: crab-apples, haws, blackberries, bullaces and elder berries. Sophie would toss in a few honeycombs and add some gallons of water, and after much glutinous bubbling the result would be carefully decanted into jam-jars, labelled with the date and the title "Hedgerow Jam", and stored on the wooden slats of the larder.

With a macabre poetic justice Adolf and Benito, the pigs, who had been fed throughout the year on the contents of the boiler, would end up in it, stewing for several days in a mixture of saltpetre, stout and molasses. The hams, pitch black and as hard as anvils, would be hung up on hooks from the kitchen ceiling.

The third purpose was for the brewing of beers and wines. Hart was the expert at this, and for a week he would leave off his job as the orchard-keeper and fossick and fidget with herbs and flowers and fruits which he would steep and stir within the enamelled bowl. After much sniffing and many tastings, Hart would have filled about two dozen large earthenware containers: ginger-beer for the children, a poisonous-looking but surprisingly pleasant beetroot wine for the adults and his own special mixture of fermented wheat, potatoes and rotten apples for carol singers, the British Legion Dinner, the Women's Institute and other riotous assemblies. The containers would seethe and bubble to each other as they stood on the brick floor of the apple store. It was generally about two months before they could be drunk.

I was reminded of all this when Cedric Cattermole, the estate agent, sent me a circular from the Common Market people about vineyards. If I wanted a vineyard, it said, I would have to register the fact by the end of the month.

There are several successful vineyards locally, producing pleasant white wines. I visited one, and then read a book on the subject. The visit impressed me, and I was fired with enthusiasm. The book depressed me, and dampened down the fire: like many technical books, it contained a list of diseases – moulds, wilts, blights and bugs – which made horrible reading. I then worked out a few costs and decided it was too expensive a gamble. However during my research I had also looked at alternative wines and brews, and it seemed to me that we were already producing many of the ingredients of these, without having to undergo the risks and expenses of planting a vineyard.

Silver Birch sap was a good example. These trees grow scattered about the estate like weeds, they have not been planted deliberately for they are usually thought of as pretty, but unproductive. The

Laplanders and Northern Russians make a wine from their sap: an average-sized birch can be tapped of about two gallons without any harm to the tree. My father, who knows both Russia and Finland well, says the wine tastes of particularly insipid tap-water, but George IV, when Prince Regent, said that it was his favourite amongst the wines. This, I thought, would help to market the drink if I tried to sell it to the public. I would call it "Queen of the Woods", the folk-lore name for the tree, and have a pretty, rustic looking label showing the Prince Regent sipping wine with a wood nymph on his knee.

The next spring, therefore, when the sap was rising, I nipped the ends off some small branches on ten trees and tied bottles over the cut ends. After I had harvested about twenty gallons I asked Hart to help me to try out different recipes. He knows three recipes, Mrs Rutland knows another, involving the addition of dandelions, and Mrs Softjoy, Monique Fewmet's vapid friend, told us of one she had learned in her wine-making classes.

By the time Matthew was telling me of his gourmets' tour, the Queen of the Woods were ready for drinking. I decided I could do what the marketing trade calls a "consumer trial", and help Matthew at the same time.

They sat in a row on one of the bench seats of Matthew's old shooting brake, an ancient Rolls Royce with wood-panelled sides and a long yellow bonnet. At first sight, they were a rum-looking trio: one was huge, another was tiny and the third was as bald as a stone. The hugeness of the huge one was not entirely because he was very fat; he was also about six foot six. He spoke in a piping treble; disconcerting as the French steam-engines whose colossal bulk was made ludicrous by their squeaky little whistles. He was something to do with the tourist board and his name was Mr Bubb.

The bald one was an expert on wine and owned a chain of restaurants in Holland. He was called Mr Van Sondvick.

The little one was our local professional sponger, Archibald fforespend. When his father was killed in the First World War, Archie inherited a long family tree, a huge empty house, and little else. He scratched a living by being a gossip columnist. The pay was not good but almost every day he could wheedle invitations to free meals, plus the best places in the theatre and at social events.

He repaid this hospitality by writing about his acquaintances with vitriolic loathing. Many of these acquaintances were so entranced and flattered by being mentioned in the newspapers that they asked him to even more parties. His career came to an end when he married his first rich wife, but scrounging is second nature to him, so even though he has now been married to four heiresses he can be found where the takings are free and lavish.

He unwound a window and goggled at me through his monocle. I noticed that it was magnifying the veins and blotches on his yellow eyeball. "Ah, dear boy," he said, "and what have you got for us . . .?"

He became distracted by Jennie walking past, holding Bumble Bee by the leading rein. She was wearing her hay-making uniform of bikini, boots and gloves.

"Hello, my dear. Are you fond of animals?"

"Well, yes," said Jennie, smiling at the kindly old gentleman.

"I'm so glad, my dear, for so am I. We must discuss our interests together. Tell me, my dear, will you make an old man very happy and dine with me tonight, and incidently are you on The Pill?"

Matthew looked glum. "Insatiable little brute," he said, "even made a pass at my Great-Aunt Tourmaline last night. She's ninety-five and has a huge white beard."

"How did dinner and breakfast go?" I asked.

"Quite well. We had dinner at home. As you know, Mrs Sudbury is a brilliant cook, and it impressed them that everything they ate was off the estate: the vegetables from the kitchen garden, the trout from the moat, the venison from the park and the pineapples from the pineapple-etum.

"Breakfast wasn't quite so successful as Archie had a hangover and the fat fellow got a kipper bone stuck down his throat."

I clambered up the flight of steps that led up to the interior of the car, and after Matthew had introduced us, I said, "You will remember that the parties of gourmets will be taken somewhere interesting in the morning, if possible somewhere to do with food. We have organised two optional visits: one is to the Colchester Oyster Fishery, the other to Daw's Hall Wildfowl Farm. We only have time to visit the bird sanctuary today, but the oyster farmer also organises lunches on his island, and we are going there after we have looked at the birds."

For some reason, Archie sniggered.

"Daw's Hall specialises in pheasants and wildfowl. I suppose you could say that they are connected with food, but I shouldn't mention the fact: it might annoy Major Grahame to have his birds thought of as mere items for the table."

Iain Grahame and his two companions, who were waiting for us behind the wire-mesh door of his enclosure, made a strange tableau. Iain had just returned from Uganda, where he had been sent by the British Government to persuade his old platoon sergeant, Idi-son-of-Amin, to stop eating one of our business-men. He had lost half a stone and the whites of his eyes kept showing.

His companions stood on either side of him.

He introduced us to the one on his right. "'Trumpy', the trumpeter bird."

Trumpy was one of the most badly made animals I ever met. His neck and head were rather like a chicken's but were covered with soft, velvety plumage. This compared incongruously with the bundle of scruffy, ragged quills which stuck out at all angles from his spheroid body. The whole ensemble teetered on long, stilt-like legs.

"He's moulting," explained Iain apologetically. "And he keeps trying to seduce anything in skirts which comes his way." Archie bridled at Iain's involuntary glance.

As if in reply, the bird cocked its head up at us, to disclose a friendly, twinkling eye, and emitted what I would call a booming honk but which Iain described as a "drunken cellist performing a vibrato on his lowest B".

Iain indicated the other creature, which was grunting comfortably by his left foot. It appeared to be an over-stuffed bolster with, at one end, a minute snout surrounded by wrinkles and, at the other end, a piece of frayed rope. "Our Vietnamese pot-bellied pig. His name is Cobus."

Our bald companion screamed with laughter and slapped his thigh. "That means 'dirty old man' in my language."

"Yes, it was named by a Dutch girl who is married to my assistant."

He led us to his pheasantry. Cobus and Trumpy, who seemed to have taken a liking to Mr Bubb, the huge man, trotted or spindle-shanked after us. We inspected a variety of birds, all of great beauty, many of extreme rarity: Tragopans with their exotic plumage speckled with sequin-like scatterings of round white spots, Argus pheasants whose ornate tails rivalled the trains of the adjacent peacocks, blue-eared pheasants with upswept "horns", cheer pheasants with hanging crests . . .

". . . and these are the rarest of the lot, Himalayan blood pheasants. It took me several years to get these. Eventually I had to go 12,000 feet up the mountains and capture them myself."

Mr Bubb peered through the netting of their pen with passionate intensity. "Fascinating," he said. "Fascinating. And how are they cooked?"

The whites of Iain's eyes flashed. "They are not. Not where I'm around," he snapped.

Mr Bubb looked disappointed, then glanced down uneasily at Cobus who was staring up at him with undisguised admiration. As the tour progressed, Mr Bubb's unease increased. Black swans floated past us, Mandarin ducks grunted, wood ducks whistled, snow geese preened; Mr Bubb seemed oblivious of the exotic life around him, all he did was to keep looking worriedly at the porcine admirer trotting at his heels, its beady little eyes filled with an expression that was near to reverence. I still remember the pig's expression as he watched us get back into the car when the visit was over: he stared at Mr Bubb with a terrible yearning. On the other hand, Mr Bubb's final hurried glimpse over his shoulder was one of deep resentment.

In the Colne estuary there is a creek called the Pyefleet Channel. It undulates between Langenhoe Marsh and Wick Marsh to the north and Mersea Island to the south. The land to either side is typical of the Essex saltings: low and level, with many islets, and mud flats which shine with a greasy wet gloss at low tide. Waders and dippers dabble and puggle for the worms and crustaceans which live in the mud, skeins of duck and geese wing high up among the ragged clouds of the cold, pallid dawns. Many people hate the marshlands. They are awed by the huge expanse of sky which arches to far-off horizons, they find cheerless the thin breeze which whines through the wiry growth on the sea walls, they are made uneasy by the taciturn abruptness of the weather-beaten people who live in the coastal villages. But, in autumn, when the sea lavender stains lilac-coloured drifts on the islands, it is beautiful; and it is impossible to forget the lonely calls of the geese and the piping of the curlews.

There is a large Nissen hut on Pewit Island. It stands on stilts to keep it clear of the high tides. It is stark and functional, which is perhaps why it merges well with its surroundings.

Christopher Kerrison, the oyster farmer, produces some of the best food in the East of England within its black-tarred walls.

His ferry is the *Saxonia*, a shrimp bawley: single-masted, cutter-rigged, with a long bow-sprit and a rust-red mainsail. We were not the only people aboard: there was a cheerful, chatty party of a dozen tourists, and the crew. Reuben, the captain, was large and grizzled-blond, like many of the marshlanders who have a mixture of Saxon and Viking in their veins. Kevin, his grandson, was wearing the traditional blue jersey, cotton trousers and high thigh-boots of the marshlanders, but had the head-phones of a boogie-pack clamped round his head.

We crossed the murky waters of the channel, landed on the island and climbed up the flight of steps which lead to the interior of the hut. Christopher Kerrison introduced himself and gave us a brief talk on his trade.

"The Colchester oyster is famous for being a particularly full-bodied, fat, juicy shellfish," he started off.

Mr Bubb licked his fat, juicy lips.

"Most of you probably know the legend that the Romans had relays of horses dashing across Europe, carrying Colchester Oysters to Rome for special feasts. I personally do not think it possible; I think it more likely that they put them in nets and hung them over the gunwales of their ships. However some people think that the Romans did not eat them fresh, but ate them putrid, with honey."

All of us, except Mr Bubb, looked slightly nauseated. Mr Bubb looked interested.

"We have a nursery for seed oysters in the Outer Hebrides. The young oysters are taken from there to Loch Ryan for fattening, and finally they come to our oyster beds here for their final growth, and to get their unique Colchester taste.

"Obviously, oysters are the biggest thing on the menu, but we also have clams, mussels, scallops, crabs, lobsters, shrimps, prawns, grey mullet, sprats and whitebait."

Ignoring the little moan of gluttony emitted by Mr Bubb, the bald Dutchman asked, "How true is it that oysters are an aphrodisiac?"

Kerrison gave a world-weary smile, as of someone who has heard something oft repeated, but before he could reply, Archie fforespend butted in.

"Don't believe it me-self," he said. "I think it's the bread and butter."

"Why?" someone asked.

"Because I only started eating oysters when I was twelve."

The furniture was simple – scrubbed wooden benches and two long tables. The food was superb. It was too good. When Mr Bubb had given a final smack to his lips, when Archie's bushy moustache had stopped undulating to his masticating, and when the Dutchman had pushed away his last emptied plate with a contented sigh, the tide had come in. "No worry," said Christopher, as we heard the sea lapping against the base of the poles upon which the hut stood. "We're used to this, it often happens. Reuben and Kevin here will give everyone a piggy-back to the boat."

The women present emitted delighted screams of scandalised surprise. Reuben and Kevin beamed affably at them.

The water was not very deep: half way up the thigh-boots of the seamen. They did not have to wade far, about a dozen yards, and the conveyers, burdened with their passengers of giggling women or grim-faced, men, soon completed their task. Finally, only the colossal bulk of Mr Bubb was left, looking stranded and forlorn on the deserted beach.

"I'll do him," said old Reuben, spitting on his hands.

"Don't be such a twit, Grandad," said Kevin. "This is a two-man job."

"I was a-hauling boats twice his weight up and down the Hard afore you was born," said the old fool defiantly.

When Bubb was finally hitched off the ground, we could see by his expression of stolid resentment that he was not pleased. We could see that Reuben was even less pleased. His eyes stood out like organ stops, veins miraculously appeared all over his forehead, the tendons and muscles on his lean old neck knotted and writhed. However, he was a powerful man, and with a determined but lurching gait he entered the water. After about five paces he stopped.

"Go on," gritted Mr Bubb, riled by the tittering and whispered comments emanating from the bawley.

. . . . Me bloody feet are stuck . . .

"I can't," gasped Reuben. "Me bloody feet are stuck." Their combined weight, which must have been about thirty stone, had driven him into the sea bed like a tent peg.

"Well, what are you going to do then?" asked Mr Bubb, somewhat fractiously.

"I dunno, boi, do I?" replied Reuben plaintively.

They stared at us in the boat.

We stared back.

Presently it became obvious that they were settling further into the briny, like a waterlogged barge. It was also obvious that Reuben was weakening. He let go of one of Mr Bubb's legs, and it flopped into the water up to the knee.

"Let go then," snarled Reuben's passenger, hanging askew, "I'll wade."

"No no, boi, don't you fret," panted the older sailor, then feeling Bubb's other leg slipping from his grip, he grabbed at it with his spare arm.

He lost his balance.

We gazed in rapt silence as the whole massive edifice turned on its pivot, almost as if in slow motion, and leaned further and further over. Mr Bubb looked like King Kong hanging on to his skyscraper. With scarcely a splash, they disappeared beneath the murky waters of the Colne estuary.

We gazed at the empty expanse of sea, horrified, but enthralled. Moments passed. A feeling of unease and doubt prevailed. Nothing appeared. Wavelets danced and glinted over the spot where the two titans had vanished.

Suddenly, with a huge swirl of foam and a bellow of rage, Mr Bubb appeared, like a harpooned whale. Reuben followed.

"Oh, dear. I'm terribly sorry," nittered Matthew. "Are you alright? What bad luck. I hope it wasn't too cold. Your suit . . ."

Mr Bubb had two options, to lose his temper, or to laugh it off. Fortunately for us, he kindly chose the latter; but I could see he was seething with suppressed rage as he stood in his socks and underpants in front of the coke stove of the Nissen hut, watching his tweeds steam dry.

Kerrison now takes his guests across in a rubber dinghy.

Monique Fewmet will do anything for Matthew. He had found it easy to persuade her to have the supper-drinks party at Hempseed Hall, and she, in her turn, had managed to persuade Mrs Softjoy to help her. We had decided to ask about twenty guests, as well as the trio of inspectors, but when we arrived, rather late, I saw that over a hundred people were already packed within the pink-painted walls of the Fewmets' drawing-room. Monique had asked fifty of her closest friends, Mrs Softjoy had invited members of her meditation and yoga classes, Matthew had asked a variety of people to whom he owed hospitality and I had asked anyone involved in the production of the food and drink.

I saw that they did not mix. Neatly suited commuters, just off their London trains, gazed with fastidious awe at the beards and beads of Mrs Softjoy's friends; the makers of cheeses and the brewers of beer smiled, with kindly disparagement, at the mincing voices of the Fewmet clan. However, the conversation was flowing, and as I jostled through the throng, phrases and comments drifted to my ears . . .

". . . I'm afraid that Tancred is not very academic, but he did get quite a good C in his O Level Constructive Beadwork . . ."

". . . Oh, you live in Peebles! You must know my cousins the Nutstones? . . . No? Well the Viviparous-Blennies? . . . No? Frankie and Titania Boddiss? . . . No? You *must* know old Sir Titus Sandstone, he owns half the county? . . . Well, the Pillweeds then? . . . not even Doreen, the Marquesa of Costa del Grott? God! You don't know anybody . . ."

". . . Now that you mention it, one of my first mistresses used to say that I reminded her of a Greek god. Poor little thing, she was so possessive. I had just to lift an eyebrow at another pretty girl and she'd go wild. Had to marry her off to yet another friend in the House of Lords, not the one who . . ."

". . . I ensure that my caviare or sables come from Russia and I take some of those dear little Militant Tendency people to see the Bolshoi every year; poor dears, they are so grateful and call me Felicity, so amusing and democratic . . ."

". . . up to his armpits in boiling goat-fat . . ."

". . . so I left the Rat Race to live closer to Nature. That is why I sold the Hall and moved into that nice little thatched cottage, and of course private education is an anachronism, the chap who took my place on the board is terribly decent, he asks me to lunch twice a year . . ."

". . . So you are a doctor, are you! Hang on a minute, I expect you'll be interested in this oddly shaped boil on the end of my . . ."

". . . and then the bastard called me a grotty little creep my God the bastard I tell you if I wasn't a man of peace I would have killed him on the spot as it is I spat yes I spat on the very place where he'd been standing the bastard *him* calling *me* a vile little pip-squeak

I'll make his pips squeak heh-heh my God the bastard let him wait I've got a long memory . . ."

". . . She was my husband's eldest cousin on his mother's side. No, I tell a lie. She was his cousin through Auntie Meg's half-sister. I first met her on a Tuesday three years ago. Or was it a Thursday? No, it was a Tuesday, because my day for the Good Samaritans used to be on Thursdays until . . ."

". . . Oh, thanking you for being alive, pardon my . . ."

". . . Golly-gosh! Miss Stipple!! You were my art mistress at St Brunhilda's. Gosh! I say! Aren't you weeny after all this time . . ."

". . . 'Robin,' I said, 'I can not and I will not forgive any unkind word about the wallpaper Raymond chose for me.' Well! He was absolutely livid . . ."

". . . so then we changed school runs and now that Rollo goes to Mrs . . ."

I was cornered by a student and his wife. At least, he said he was a student, but he was in his late forties. He wore a quilted anorak, zipped up to his Adam's-apple, and shorts. From these, sinewy legs emerged. They disappeared into a pair of sandals and re-emerged as two bunches of gnarled toes. His wife was dressed in an embroidered smock which, I was told, was the day-to-day garb of the labouring folk of Upper Silesia. Its innocent gaudiness was offset by the menace of her beetling brows and the severity of the iron-grey hair strained back into a small, hard bun. This nodule was kept in shape with an arrangement made of a wooden skewer and an embossed leather butterfly.

They said that they wanted my opinion on stubble-burning and the preservation of hedgerows. My opinion generally agreed with theirs, which was just as well, as she didn't wait to listen to it, but told me her own. Her accent, as well as her smock, originated from one of the innermost recesses of Europe: ". . . and so zer peoples who are burnink stubbles should be roasted alive in zeir own flames and then sent to a penal colony for zer hopelessly insane," she concluded.

Her husband stared down fondly at her. "She has a great sense of humour," he explained.

She nodded in surly agreement. "Yaas, zat is true. Always I am laughink and makink funny sayinks."

Our conversation was hampered by the vocal intrusions from something which hung in a bag, like a chrysalis, from the aged student's neck. Finally, even he was exasperated by its mewlings, and snatching a limp asparagus sandwich from a passing plate he plugged it into the gummy opening of the baby's mouth.

I sidled off as this unattractive process was taking place and tried to barge through the mob to the trestle table which held the samples of home-made wines, including my bottles of Queen of the Woods. Archie fforespend suddenly appeared in front of me. Already the glass in his hand was almost empty.

"Isn't that Cecily Westly-Waterless?" he said. "Bloody pretty gal, in her time. I'll go and talk to her. Meanwhile, dear boy, get me a different drink . . . God knows what I'm drinking at the moment, it smells like a French army latrine and tastes like stewed seaweed."

I met Mrs Rutland at the trestle table. She was fussing over the bottles: picking them up, reading their labels, and putting them down with a worried expression. "I think I made a mistake," she said. "You asked me to bring a sample of my broad-bean wine and I think I've brought my constipation cure instead." Dominie, next to me, blenched. Last time we had seen this example of Mrs Rutland's brewing, the bottle had exploded . . . anyone who drank it was glued to the mahogany for three days.

"On the other hand," she continued, pleased, "my recipe for Queen of the Woods is the most popular." I was not surprised: her dandelion petals had dyed it to a beautiful golden yellow, and it had a mild, evocative taste combined with a sharp alcoholic smack.

I scooped up a tumbler-full of the wine and went up to Miss Westly-Waterless. She is as thin as a rail and six foot two. She looked down at me along the hooked bridge of her nose and said, cynically, "I imagine that I have been asked to this frightful party because Matthew owes me a dinner. I only accepted because the Rutlands said that I was needed."

Archie fforespend breezed up. "Ah," he said, "it's dear old Cecily." He coiled his arm round her tightly corseted waist.

"Go away," she said. "Don't touch me, you lascivious little beast. You were terrible as a little boy, you were repulsive as a man and now you're vile as a senile old fool. You are smelly, old and ugly. I've never liked you and I never will. Keep your filthy, clammy, lecherous fingers off me and *go away*."

Archie noticed my sympathetic glance. "I like her," he said

simply, gazing with admiration at her departing back. "She is so inscrutable."

The party was nearly over. The last chop from the barbecued suckling pig had been gnawed, the Stilton soufflé had been swallowed. Mrs Softjoy weaved up to me. She held the bottle of Mrs Rutland's constipation cure in one hand, a wine glass in the other. The bottle was empty.

"I've been a very naughty girl, very naughty, very naughty indeed. Naughty me, but I couldn't resist this delicious liqueur of Mrs Rutland's. I expect I shall feel sorry, later."

"I expect you will," I agreed, and set off to assemble the trio of judges for their journey back to my house.

As usual, the kitchen was slightly chaotic: someone had trodden on one of Bert-worm's ears and he had bitten Potter in retaliation. Alfie, the bantam who had been hatched on the Aga and now thought he was a dog, had chased Pandora the cat out of her basket, and Mr Whippletree had arrived to say that he had taken samples from Little Kate, who had had bad indigestion.

"Good-bye," I shouted to the trio, who were standing by the door, looking bemused. "My wife has packed you something to keep you cheerful during your journey back to London."

I picked up a box from the table, pressed it into Archie's greedy hands, and ushered them out of the house.

"I must go, too," said Mr Whippletree, a few minutes later, as he drained the last dregs of his whisky. "Where's my box of samples? I left it on the table."

"What was in it?" Dominie asked him.

"A stuffed ferret, a bottle of preserved frogs, three close-up photographs of a hamster's bottom and the samples of Little Kate's dung."

"Ah, here it is," said Dominie, spying the corner of a box half hidden by a carelessly tossed dish cloth.

"Same size, but looks different," said Mr Whippletree.

He opened it.

In it were a dozen smoked salmon sandwiches, two bottles of Pouilly Fumée and a corkscrew.

CHAPTER 14

The Show

He saith among the trumpets, Ha, ha.
Job 39 xxv

They came from the far west – where the Colne River seeps unobtrusively out of the ground near Steeple Bumpstead – to the far east, where the muddy waters, having squeezed past Rat Island and Brightlingsea, flow out into the North Sea between the marshes of St Osyth on one side and the Island of Mersea on the other. Horses and hamsters, Carnival Queens and tractor salesmen, growers of huge onions or breeders of spruce little bantams, oyster farmers from the saltings and bell-ringers from the parishes, herdsmen of geese or of sheep, hedge-layers and glassblowers: all had come to compete or show their skills or their wares, or merely to stare.

We arrived very early at the Colne Valley Show. The morning mist had not yet cleared from the adjacent osier plantation and the cattle were still motionless in the dew-sodden water meadows, but, when our horse-box trundled up the central ride of the show ground, we saw that preparations were in full swing. We parked in the horse lines. Dominie and Jennie started titivating the show ponies, the girls tittupped off on their riding ponies, to warm them up before their competitions began. The boys began to cook breakfast, their second, on the stove in the galley of the horse-box. Monk, Hart and I wandered off to see the show coming to life.

With many a cry of "Easy now", "Pull here, Bert", "Down a

bit", "Up again", "Not there, you silly bugger", the main tent was being hoisted like a vast grey elephant staggering to its feet. Several smaller tents were already pitched and people were entering them with armloads of produce. Women were darting critical glances at each other's cakes or embroidery. Men were heaving colossal marrows or bearing tiny button-holes, or carrying, as carefully as they would carry their grandchildren, bowls of roses, bunches of chrysanthemums, carrots a foot long, potatoes scrubbed till they glowed, clutches of eggs and bottles of sloe gin. Other, even smaller tents, bulged and hummed with activity and noise. In one a voice was heard droning ". . . two thousand five hundred and sixty eight, two thousand five hundred and sixty nine, two thousand five hundred and sixty . . . or is it seventy? Oh bother, oh bother, I hate these beans, I hate them I hate them I hate them. Who'll want to guess how many there are anyway, how boring boring, oh blast, oh well . . . one, two, three, four, five . . ." Another tent was marked "HOME MADE WINES, JAMS, PICKLES, SAVOURY SAUCES", and from it could be heard the nitter and cackle of gossips as they compared each other's husbands, ailments, neighbours and other inconveniences.

A corner of the show ground had been set aside for the fun-fair. Coconuts were being glued into place in the coconut shy, the sights of the air-guns in the shooting gallery were being given a cautionary twist to ensure no one would harm the lines of clay pipes set out as targets. In his booth, Mahommed MacGregor, the palmist, was dusting his crystal ball. Beside a small roundabout, burdened with a stampede of crudely carpentered ponies, a village band was recovering from the strains of practising "The Foggy Foggy Dew" and "The Old Grey Mare". Cornets, tubas and saxophones drooled tiredly from opened taps, violins gave the occasional screech or whimper, a flute was apparently having its neck wrung and the big drummer had pressed his ear to his instrument, which he kept giving a resounding wallop.

The conductor tapped his music stand sternly with his baton. A respectful silence fell. Instruments were hoisted into position. Chests were expanded, breaths were held. The conductor put one finger cautiously to his pursed lips. He gently raised the baton.

The baton descended.

All hell broke loose.

The very sky seemed to shimmer with noise, and Nature halted

in her tracks with appalled surprise. It sounded like the whole
Siamese army charging into battle: the elephants screaming with
rage and the fighting cats howling with blood-lust from the armed
shoulders of their warrior owners.

The shrieks of the brass section blared above the yowls of the
woodwind, the thunderous clattering of the side-drums contrasted
frenziedly to the muffled, irregular heart-beats of the big drum
and the startlingly sudden clashes of the cymbals. Sweat began to
pour off scarlet faces and soak the gold-embroidered collars. Eyes
glared in exultant concentration. The conductor, his arms flailing
as if he were playing tennis against a score of people at once,
allowed a faint expression of gratified approval to adorn his
face.

Amidst the hubbub and the din one began to discern the individual noise-maker. There was Herman the German, he had been
a prisoner of war locally and when the war ended he stayed and
started a successful little clock-making business, he stared pop-eyed
as he grappled with his tuba as if its coils were attempting to
strangle him. There was another "foreigner", Dai Plimsoles, the
harpist – he had never seen a harp before leaving the Vale of
Llangollen, but he had become besottedly Celtic since then and
was determined to show the bloody Anglo-Saxons that his national
instrument could hold its own in any company: the strings of his
harp thrummed and vibrated under his fingers like the vocal cords
of a brontosaurus hollering for its mate. Other fingers, those of
Hot-Hands Honeyball, the village Romeo, were being worked up
and down his saxophone in a way that made some of the onlooking
maidens blush in recollection. Inaudible amidst the uproar but
unaware of the fact, was our local knacker, crouching over a tiny
triangle, with his eyes riveted to his score sheet. Somehow he was
able to connect its neatly printed hieroglyphics with the bedlam
around him and occasionally his calloused fingers would delicately
flick a small steel rod upon his instrument.

The last note of the finale blared into the tormented air, the
players leant back, panting; the conductor nodded benignly at
them: "Not bad, boys. I reckon we've perfected 'Come into the
Garden, Maud'. We'll rest a bit and then whilst we're still in the
mood we'll try 'Tit-willow'."

We walked on, our ears ringing. The lethargic drifting of the
early arrivals had now become a bustle as later, more urgent people

arrived. Conveyances full of livestock kept rumbling past: cattle, pigs or sheep in huge transporters, goats in be-wheeled hutches, domestic pets in screened-off sections at the back of cars. A line of traction and other steam-powered engines panted through the main entrance. Brewers and caterers began to deliver their goods at the appropriate tents. The first spectators arrived, gawping at the bustle; the first dog-fight, the first chase after an escaped bullock and finally, to show that we had at last started, the first statement over the loudspeaker asking if Mr or Mrs Edwin Scatterwell could go to the St John's Ambulance Brigade whence they could recover their lost child, Marygold.

The commercial section began to operate. It consisted of a line of tents of which the first was one of the busiest. It was selling farm produce: in their dormitory of pine-wood crates the ruddy cheeks of Beauty of Bath and Tydeman's Early Worcester glowed upon their straw pillows; edifices built from jars towered beside them, glowing with the amber lights of honey and the sombre rubies, emeralds and topazes of home-made jams; a large trestle table was ablaze with flowers; strings of dried mushrooms and plaits of onions wreathed the tent poles: sacks of potatoes and of maize were being sold from a lorry parked beside the tent. The two bear-like shapes of the salesmen ceaselessly weighed, measured and sold, whilst a third hulk sat in a corner, his vast fingers deftly busy with wires and flowers as he made button-holes and nose-gays.

"Where's Chipper?" Monk asked him.

"Dad's by the main ring. You'll not see him far from the horses today."

We moved on, down the row of tents. In some, people were at work: Mr Kimberwick, the saddler, cutting and stitching amidst his festoons of bridles, leaches, belts and traces; Brigadier Doxon, the potter, balming himself up to the elbows in sticky clay, to the envious admiration of a group of onlooking schoolboys; a nondescript bundle of dun-coloured textiles, knitted, woven and, chiefly, crocheted, which had sprouted a small pair of nimble white hands that twiddled over the intricacies of a spinning wheel. In a corner a little figure clacked at a hand loom, a sign outside their tent said:

MS A. GROSPOTTLE & PARTNER FABRICS
SPUN, DYED AND MANUFACTURED ALL BY HAND
USING TYME–TESTED METHODS

Free leaflets   *Stop factory farming*
Say 'No' to nuclear power   *Ban the bomb*

I picked up a shawl, the pattern of which I recognised. A rayon label on its corner declared that it had been imported from Taiwan by Silas Cragthorn & Son.

An extra-large tent bore a banner on which was emblazoned "J. L. FLEAME & SON, MILLERS"; inside could be discerned sacks and bushel-measures in wickerwork, a large working-table in the centre bearing a heap of papers on the left, a pair of scales on the right and a "pending" tray in the middle, empty except for a sleeping cat.

An open shed attracted us by its large encirclement of spectators and its noisy emission of metallic tappings and batterings. I stood on Monk's ferret box to look over the crowd and saw a line of glowing hearths, beside each of which stood a farrier and a horse: the shoeing competition was in progress. Mr Dewbit wandered up and down looking important – he was judging today, not competing. A cacophony of shrill yaps marked the site of another competition and we went over to investigate. A race-track had been marked out on the swarth, about sixty yards long by ten wide. At the starting end there was a line of numbered boxes, like kennels with wire doors. As we waited for the next race Matthew came lounging up to us

"I'll give you 4 to 5 on Peregrine Percy and odds on for Mrs Rosemead's Fireball Toothslasher the Third."

We ignored his urgings. Suddenly a tawny bundle of fur tied on to a string shot away from the kennels, and simultaneously their doors flew open and the air was filled with screams of encouragement and excited yapping as three scotties, a tiny Yorkshire terrier with its hair in ribbons, a heavily panting bull terrier, four Jack Russells and a mean-eyed Manchester terrier raced, waddled or minced, depending on their natures and waistlines, up the track. The Manchester terrier, Fireball Toothslasher, was the easy winner, two of the Jack Russells started to fight and were promptly dowsed with a bucket kept by as an instant peacemaker. During the fracas the effete Yorkshire terrier tip-toed round the milling

mob of dogs and owners, found the artificial rabbit in its lair, a
shoe box, and savaged it.

It was noon. Dominie and Jennie were exultantly pointing out the
scarlet roundels of two first-prize rosettes, grieving that it was
only because of a minor technicality that another showed the blue
of a second prize, and were shaking their heads in sorrowful
sympathy at the ignorance, bigotry and personal bias which had
caused a judge to give only a "highly commended" rosette to
another pony. The girls had been presented with the rosettes they
had been expecting for their riding, the boys had vanished with a
drift of friends. Tony Crisp and I went off to the stockmen's tent
for a drink.

It was full of raucous amiability: friend shouting at friend,
helpless guffawing, vapid smiles and urgent commands to the
barmaids for yet more drinks. There was no aggression or voice
raised in anger, the fiery temper of our ancestors: Boudicca,
Caradoc and Brithnoth has been diluted by the more pacific blood
of Flemish and Huguenot weavers, Frisian pig-breeders, Dutch
market-gardeners, herdsmen from the lowlands of Scotland and
stockbrokers from the highlands of Harrow. Everyone stood gossiping in groups, and I tried to analyse what made it so obvious
what their occupations were: did the cattle-drovers have a slight
air of careworn pride and did their coats have that extra-blue
whiteness; were the horsemen more abrupt in their movements
and did they have a way of glancing about from the corners of
their eyes; were the shepherds more silent than the rest of us, and
the pigmen more merry; were the poultry farmers, with whom
Tony Crisp went over to confer, more clinical and brisk, were the
gooseherds rather more dishevelled than average; did the breeders
of rabbits and other small furry creatures tend towards gins and
tonic, the goatherds to eccentric mixtures like lime and shandy
and the heavy-horsemen and drivers to porters and black beer?

I left Tony Crisp gossiping and went off to the more staid and
quieter confines of the Country Landowners' tent where assorted
aunts and ancient squires sat on chintz-covered chairs and nibbled
sandwiches. There was a bar in the corner, it was propping up a
leash of people: Matthew, heavily tweeded, Archie fforespend and
Major-General Sir Alfred Heavyside-Guestingthorpe. We sipped at
our drinks and watched the tent filling. Lunch was already being
served, and the parade of horse-drawn vehicles was imminent: the

former attraction was chiefly of interest to harassed women with whining children, the latter to the rest of us, so we left the tent for the enclave between it and the main ring, from which the last cow was plodding.

Presently there was a tootle from a coaching-horn blown by a man in green livery who then, after a few lugubrious bellows of "Oyez", announced the next parade.

First in line was a team of Suffolk Punches, their hides gleaming like polished conkers in the sunlight, their colossal heads nodding in purposeful unison as they paced forward with a slow, high-stepping stride. As they approached, their necks seemed to rear up in broad, muscled arches and we could feel the power radiate from their presence. Their driver was a massively bearded market-gardener. Posed statuesquely on his seat, high above the waggon, his only movements were the twitching of his fingers on the reins and the roving of his eyes. Behind the team of four was a team of three, a triangular formation known as a "unicorn". This is difficult to drive if the leader is flighty, as she was, being attracted by the randy screeches of a stallion in the next show-ring. The driver was a youth who had obviously taken on more than he could easily handle, and he was scarlet with embarrassment and effort as his team cavorted and bounded past the grandstand. The next team of Suffolks was owned by a farmer. The whole family sat in a gleaming row on the front seat: the farmer immaculate from his brown bowler to his gaitered legs; his wife in her best twinset and beads, her pinched face dwarfed by her hat, a weird concoction of feathers and flowers bound together with pink raffia; the three scrubbed children of diminishing size, sizzling with repressed pride and affection at the massive backs below them. The eldest son, whose nine years weighed heavily on him that day, occasionally called out in an important pipe: "Steady on, Annabelle, up a bit, Dash. Don't lean on Diamond, Blazer." This had an effect both gratifying and irritating on his father, who eventually said, "Quiet, Gladwin." The horses took no notice, they were behaving impeccably, anyway. Their cart was a superb harvest waggon, painted green and red and with a yellow notice inscribed on its rear board saying HEBIDIAH HARDCROFT & SONS, SLOUGHHOLLOW FARM.

The team of shires which came next was of such magnificence that even old Amos Quartermain the horseman, who had just joined us for a glass of Three Colnes, could scarce forbear to nod in resigned approval, though he considered the Suffolk to be the only sensible horse to use. Although the shires had the same sized heads and hooves as the Suffolk, they loomed about a hand higher. They were totally black except for white socks which rippled in great plumes at each thunderous step. As they passed, their bodies seemed like swaying barges riding out on a sea of foam, and the jingle and clash of harness and chain added to the impression that they were something more than mere domesticated animals. Above the heaving sea of muscle, high up in the driver's seat, sat one Arnold Pipkin, once known as "the Weed of Pebworth Secondary Mod", but now known as "Head Horseman to Messrs Flowermead, Silverball and Nephew Limited" or, alternatively, as "Sir".

Below the large bowler hat which seemed to be balanced on his bat-like ears, his small eyes glittered as he mapped out his route. His receding chin disclosed a ratty pair of upper teeth and the whole rodent effect was accentuated by his long thin body being tightly encased in an overcoat which stretched from the stock round his scrawny neck down to his boots.

He looked magnificent.

"That's my grandson, Arnold," screeched old Mrs Pipkin's voice from the centre of the crowd. "COOeee, Arn, we're here." There was no indication that the driver had heard, as his team, with all sixteen feet pounding in unison, swung away from the entrance gate and into the centre of the ring.

Next were the brewery drays, as immaculate as ever – Young's, Mann's, Courage's and Whitbread's – then the huge green and red pantechnicon of Williams and Griffins of Colchester, the tiny milk-float of George Junkett, the coach, traps and dog-carts of Mr Ryan's Driving Club and, finally, its chimney sending forth a cloud of black smoke, a gypsy caravan pulled by an affable cob and driven by a blonde in plum-coloured velvet. The first prize must be generous, we agreed, if Rufus had bothered to move from his camp, if only for a day,

It was nearly time for my lunch, and I went, slightly guiltily because of my indolence, back to the bustle of our horse-box.

Jennie was unravelling the plaits on one horse, the girls were cleaning and oiling the hooves of another, Dominie was telling the boys where to put the rugs and the food for the picnic. I opened a couple of wine bottles – as if by magic we were surrounded with gossiping friends all with glasses in their hands.

Captain Firecrest arrived, looked dispassionately at the milling crowd and observed acidly: "They were as fed horses in the morning: everyone neighed after his neighbour's wife!" and added "Jeremiah, chapter five, verse eight." He opened up the handle of his umbrella, sat on it, took a tumbler full of Ridley's pale ale and gazed with fastidious disgust at Charlie who was packing his face with chipolata sausages and Candy who was meticulously making potato-crisp and peanut butter sandwiches for herself and Bert-worm.

A familiar yet unexpected figure suddenly materialised round the horse-box and stood smiling down at us.

"Sergeant Skerrick! What are you doing here?"

"Someone told me that my old charger, Flint, the one I rode during the coronation, is still alive and acting as companion to a string of racehorses somewhere locally. I just want to say 'hello' to her again, and see she's well cared for."

Captain Firecrest looked up.

"Flint: a dappled grey mare with a star and oblique blaze and a slight limp on the fore off?" he asked.

Sergeant Skerrick looked stricken. "The face is the old face, but the limp sounds new."

Captain Firecrest said, "I'll take you later to see if it's her."

It was after lunch; everyone had bustled off. I went and joined a clutch of bored-looking fathers who were leaning lethargically against the white-painted rail of the smallest ring. Within it, a group of tiny Thelwell-type ponies were practising jumping over poles set horizontally a foot above the ground. The men were discussing the most likely winners: Rosanna, a rangy brunette, looked the most promising – she had the pace and a pleasing open stride – but Anne, a platinum palomino, although slightly handicapped by carrying a bit more weight, was a natural jumper with an unexpected spring to her leaping; Pru was the dark horse, no one knew her form (most of it was hidden under several cardigans and a heavy pair of jodhpurs), but she had a brisk pace and bold, determined features. The ponies that these – and other – mothers towed behind them looked less determined and some of the riders were distinctly wobbly and apprehensive.

Amongst the rag-tag motley of ponies and parents there stood, like an iceberg surrounded by a school of seals, Lady Glaister, her drooping eyelids hiding eyes as keen as icicles, her profile like a Nefertiti carved out of snow. Even the Shetland Ponies quailed at her coldly critical gaze, as I used to, twenty-five years earlier, whenever the music of a Paul Jones stopped and I found myself facing the disdainful glance of Grizelda Aigrish. Her gaze drifted over the assembled multitude like the north wind blowing over lemmings on the tundra and then froze upon a pony and rider. Her shooting-stick rose like a javelin, its needle tip pointing accusingly at them: "That child has been sewn to its saddle, unstitch it."

Meekly and blushingly the attendant mother, Mrs Softjoy, unpicked the shamefaced infant from its artificially secure roost.

Lady Glaister's voice cut like a whiplash once more: "Right, everyone in the waiting pen except for the first competitor; we will proceed."

Boredom and resignation dampened the spirits of the fathers once more: the arrival of Monique Fewmet's husband, squiffy, changed the air of gloom into one of merriment, his bottle of whisky rather than his personality being the chief reason. Faces cleared, cries of encouragement rose as ponies sped past with bobbing loads and panting handlers. Egged on by their punters' exhortations, Anne bounded higher and higher and Pru's teeth grew more and more gritted. I saw my fifty pence on Rosanna slipping away. My hopes were finally dashed when she went sailing with gazelle-like grace over a jump, leaving her pony disconsolate and stubbornly rooted to the spot on the other side. Cheers and spontaneous clappings broke out from the fathers at the magnificence of Rosanna's leap, her handler bowed modestly to the rest of us in acknowledgement.

From the official loudspeaker I could hear the smoothly drawling voice of Cedric Cattermole calling out the winners of the driver and passenger class:

"First: Major and Mrs Booth in their coach and pair. Second: Mr Michael Ryan and his grandson Ernest in his dog-cart. Third: the Honorable Pamela Pennyworth and her husband Cyril in their hansom cab. Will Group-Captain Fingersides and Councillor Courtauld please go to the small collecting ring to judge the beauties for the Show Queen."

Ms O'Toole, the gym mistress, was in charge of this deadly

event. By the glowering of her eyes beneath the single black stripe of bristle which served as eyebrows, she disapproved of it.

"Apt," she said nastily as the Group-Captain skidded on a cow-pat, "that this was last used for the assembly of livestock."

The airman and I were placed side-by-side on a couple of chairs in the middle of the ring, where we sat in sheepish silence, subjected to the sardonic gaze and insulting ribaldry of the crowd which encircled the area. A small tent in front of us emitted a continuous cascade of giggles and tittering, odd bulges kept protruding from its side. Finally, from it, a collection of callow mawkins were led out, wearing bathing suits and glassy smiles and teetering on high heels. I sat there, being watched as I watched, and grew increasingly embarrassed. The Group-Captain – or "Grope"-Captain, as he was known by the girls of the town near his aerodrome – was a small, spare man with a questing, eager head like a hungry cockerel. He grew furtively excited and kept fiddling with his tie, clearing his throat and crossing and uncrossing his legs. Ms O'Toole led each girl up to us in disapproving silence and then glowered at us whilst the girl turned solemnly before us on her axis like a doner kebab on a spit, being roasted by the hot fire of Fingersides' eyes. Ms O'Toole then barked four questions at each girl: the answers, like the questions, were usually the same:

"What are your hobbies?"

"I like to go horse-riding and to travel."

"What is your ambition when you start work?"

"I want to look after children or be a vet."

"What would you do if you won the football pools?"

"I'd take my mum to a Barry Manilow concert and buy my boyfriend a new crash helmet for his motor-bike."

"Why do you use Teen-times Foundation and Cleansing Creams?"

"I use Teen-times Foundation and Cleansing Creams because they clear up my spots and give my skin that English-rose glow and freshness."

Fingersides and I could not agree on the winner: he liked a small, fluffy blonde with a squeaky voice and huge bosoms; I liked a tall Indian who refused to exchange her sari for a bathing suit and said that her ambition was to have eight sons and one daughter, an answer which caused Ms O'Toole to blush. We finally compromised on a merry girl with a toothily infectious grin and a superb

. . . . I grew increasingly embarrassed . . .

cascade of hair and then we left, under the hostile scowls of the parents and boyfriends of those who hadn't won.

I wandered back past the livestock tents and show-ring. I peered at the sheep, talked to the geese, avoided the domesticated pets, scratched a few pigs in the small of the back and stopped at an enclave where there was a dog show.

What was that small, maned lion tinged with copper like the rays of a setting sun, with the arrogant, high-stepping stride of a hackney, with flashing eyes like a dragon; whose curled tail was carried like a banner over the billowy tresses of mane and ears, whose toes had long plumes like egret feathers and whose snowy fangs bared arrogantly when any lesser breed impudently approached?

It was The-August-Personage-in-Jade.

Millicent looked as vacant as ever.

I went on to the goat tents where some of the nanny-goats were being milked into tiny pails by loose girls in tight jerseys, had a look at a bee-keeping demonstration and wondered if I should start up a bee farm, and finally arrived at the horse-box. The only thing I did not go and see was the ring where Dominie had the ponies. I feel so futile and useless, standing by the edge of the ring and seeing her running round trying to show off her ponies at their best, or standing in the line hoping to be called forward by the judge; I'd rather stay away and hear about it later.

We had a mass of rosettes, Jennie was proudly arranging them on a string which she had tied from one side of the windscreen to the other.

"Not bad," I agreed, "but each of those useless bits of silk must have cost a fortune in food and vet's bills and time and effort."

"Money isn't everything," replied Dominie. "Sometimes things are worth doing just for the satisfaction of a job well done and for a creation you can be proud of."

I looked at the pleased and contented faces around me, the glossy, healthy ponies and the row of rosettes.

"Perhaps you're right," I said.

The calm stillness of evening pervaded the show grounds. The crowds had gone, the stalls were empty. A faint hum of conversation and laughter still bumbled from the tents of the stockmen, but sounded muffled and afar. Someone was whistling as he bedded down his beloved Punches in the lines of heavy horse. The clank of pails clattered from the distant cattle-stalls.

Our horse-box was ready to go. Contented munching came from the ponies' partition, there was a rustling over my head in the Luton where the children were jostling for the best view through the dormer window. Dominie sat next to me in the driving cab, half asleep; Jennie, next to her, lovingly arranged the garland of rosettes that hung across the top of the windscreen. Before I pressed the starter button of the rackety engine I glanced along the gravelled drive to my right. Only three figures were visible, walking slowly between the tents, towards the sunset: a very, very ancient dappled grey with a slight limp in her off foreleg and, supporting her on either side, two old men. One, clothed in black, was speaking; his words were just audible floating triumphantly into the twilit air:

"Hast thou given the horse strength? hast thou clothed his neck with thunder?

Canst thou make him afraid as a grasshopper? the glory of his nostrils is terrible.

He paweth in the valley, and rejoiceth in his strength: he goeth on to meet the armed men.

He mocketh at fear, and is not affrighted: neither turneth he back from the sword.

The quiver rattleth against him, the glittering spear and the shield.

He swalloweth the ground with fierceness and rage: neither believeth he that it is the sound of the trumpet.

He saith among the trumpets, Ha, ha; and he smelleth the battle afar off, the thunder of the captains, and the shouting."

The three shadows merged, and faded into the dusk: it was time to go home.

BIBLIOGRAPHY

HORSE & PONY

Dealing with Horses. J. F. Kelly (Stanley Paul & Co. Ltd, 1961)

Driving. The Duke of Beaufort KG (Longmans, Green & Co., 1890)

Encyclopaedia of Driving. Sallie Walrond (Horse Drawn Carriages Ltd, 1974)

Horse Breeding & Stud Management. Henry Wynmalen MFH (J. A. Allan & Co. Ltd, 1971)

Riding for Ladies. Mrs Power O'Donoghue (W. Thacker & Co., 1887)

Stable Management & Exercise. Captain M. Horace Hayes, FRCVS (Stanley Paul, 1900/1925)

The Amateur Horse Breeder. Ann C. Leighton Hardman (Pelham Books, 1970)

The Encyclopaedia of the Horse. Ed. Lt. Col. C. E. G. Hope/G. N. Jackson (Ebury Press & Pelham Books, 1973)

The Farm Waggon of England & Wales. James Arnold (John Baker, 1969)

The English Gypsy Caravan. C. H. Ward-Jackson & Denis E. Harvey (David & Charles, 1973)

The Heavy Horse, Its Harness & Harness Decoration. Terry Keegan (Pelham Books, 1973)

The Horse. Ed. Candida Geddes (Octopus Books Ltd, 1978)

The Horse, with a Treatise on Draught. (Baldwin & Cradock, 1831)

The Horseman's Companion. Ed. Dorian Williams (Eyre Methuen, 1978)

The Horseman's Vade Mecum. (Adam & Charles Black, 1971)

The International Horseman's Dictionary. Charles Stratton (Hamlyn, 1975)

The Kingdom of the Horse. H-H. Isenbart and E. M. Buhrer (C. J. Bucher, 1969)

The Way of the Horse. Marguerite de Beaumont (J. A. Allan & Co. Ltd, 1953/1972)

Through the Stable and Saddle Room. Major Arthur T. Fisher (Richard Bentley & Son, 1891)

Veterinary Notes for Horse Owners. Captain M. Horace Hayes, FRCVS (Stanley Paul, 1877/1971).

Welsh Ponies & Cobs. Dr Wynne Davies (J. A. Allen & Co. Ltd, 1980)

GENERAL

An Axe, A Spade and Ten Acres. George Courtauld (Secker & Warburg, 1983)

Brewer's Dictionary of Phrase & Fable. (Cassell & Co. Ltd.)

Flying Feathers. Iain Grahame (Fontana, 1978)

Pears Encyclopaedia of Myths & Legends (Northern Europe). Sheila Savill (Pelham Books, 1977)

Primrose McConnell's Agricultural Notebook. Ed. Dr Ian Moore (Newnes-Butterworth, 1883/1977)

Taboo. Franz Steiner (Cohen & West Ltd, 1956)

The Gentleman Cook. Ed. Diana Tritton (Distressed Gentlefolk's Aid Association, 1984)

The Golden Bough (abridged edition). Sir James George Frazer, FRS, FBA (Macmillan & Co. Ltd, 1953).

Rural England. H. Rider Haggard (Longmans, Green & Co., 1902)